CAREER EXAMINATION SERIES

THIS IS YOUR **PASSBOOK**® FOR ...

COMPUTER ASSOCIATE (SOFTWARE)

NATIONAL LEARNING CORPORATION®
passbooks.com

PASSBOOK® SERIES

THE *PASSBOOK® SERIES* has been created to prepare applicants and candidates for the ultimate academic battlefield – the examination room.

At some time in our lives, each and every one of us may be required to take an examination – for validation, matriculation, admission, qualification, registration, certification, or licensure.

Based on the assumption that every applicant or candidate has met the basic formal educational standards, has taken the required number of courses, and read the necessary texts, the *PASSBOOK® SERIES* furnishes the one special preparation which may assure passing with confidence, instead of failing with insecurity. Examination questions – together with answers – are furnished as the basic vehicle for study so that the mysteries of the examination and its compounding difficulties may be eliminated or diminished by a sure method.

This book is meant to help you pass your examination provided that you qualify and are serious in your objective.

The entire field is reviewed through the huge store of content information which is succinctly presented through a provocative and challenging approach – the question-and-answer method.

A climate of success is established by furnishing the correct answers at the end of each test.

You soon learn to recognize types of questions, forms of questions, and patterns of questioning. You may even begin to anticipate expected outcomes.

You perceive that many questions are repeated or adapted so that you can gain acute insights, which may enable you to score many sure points.

You learn how to confront new questions, or types of questions, and to attack them confidently and work out the correct answers.

You note objectives and emphases, and recognize pitfalls and dangers, so that you may make positive educational adjustments.

Moreover, you are kept fully informed in relation to new concepts, methods, practices, and directions in the field.

You discover that you arre actually taking the examination all the time: you are preparing for the examination by "taking" an examination, not by reading extraneous and/or supererogatory textbooks.

In short, this PASSBOOK®, used directedly, should be an important factor in helping you to pass your test.

COMPUTER ASSOCIATE (SOFTWARE)

DUTIES

Computer Associates (Software) under direct supervision, with moderate latitude for independent initiative and judgment, are responsible for the analysis, design, development, implementation, troubleshooting, enhancement, maintenance and security of database management systems, operating systems, data communication systems, applications, websites, and/or related software functions; may supervise staff performing these functions. All Computer Associates (Software) perform related work.

SCOPE OF THE EXAMINATION

The multiple-choice test is designed to assess the extent to which candidates have certain knowledge and abilities determined to be important to the performance of the tasks of a Computer Associate (Software). Task areas to be tested are as follows: database management systems, operating systems and user roles, data communication systems, system applications, mobile applications, and web based environments.

The test may include questions on: knowledge of software principles including applications and operating systems; knowledge of the systems development life cycle (SDLC) including flow creation, data mapping, system analysis, database structures and data entities; knowledge of coding principles; knowledge of diagnosing software issues (e.g., system abends, debugging, missing files, etc.); standards of proper employee ethical conduct; and other related areas. The test may also include questions requiring the use of any of the following abilities: written expression, problem sensitivity, number facility, deductive reasoning, and critical thinking.

HOW TO TAKE A TEST

I. YOU MUST PASS AN EXAMINATION

A. WHAT EVERY CANDIDATE SHOULD KNOW

Examination applicants often ask us for help in preparing for the written test. What can I study in advance? What kinds of questions will be asked? How will the test be given? How will the papers be graded?

As an applicant for a civil service examination, you may be wondering about some of these things. Our purpose here is to suggest effective methods of advance study and to describe civil service examinations.

Your chances for success on this examination can be increased if you know how to prepare. Those "pre-examination jitters" can be reduced if you know what to expect. You can even experience an adventure in good citizenship if you know why civil service exams are given.

B. WHY ARE CIVIL SERVICE EXAMINATIONS GIVEN?

Civil service examinations are important to you in two ways. As a citizen, you want public jobs filled by employees who know how to do their work. As a job seeker, you want a fair chance to compete for that job on an equal footing with other candidates. The best-known means of accomplishing this two-fold goal is the competitive examination.

Exams are widely publicized throughout the nation. They may be administered for jobs in federal, state, city, municipal, town or village governments or agencies.

Any citizen may apply, with some limitations, such as the age or residence of applicants. Your experience and education may be reviewed to see whether you meet the requirements for the particular examination. When these requirements exist, they are reasonable and applied consistently to all applicants. Thus, a competitive examination may cause you some uneasiness now, but it is your privilege and safeguard.

C. HOW ARE CIVIL SERVICE EXAMS DEVELOPED?

Examinations are carefully written by trained technicians who are specialists in the field known as "psychological measurement," in consultation with recognized authorities in the field of work that the test will cover. These experts recommend the subject matter areas or skills to be tested; only those knowledges or skills important to your success on the job are included. The most reliable books and source materials available are used as references. Together, the experts and technicians judge the difficulty level of the questions.

Test technicians know how to phrase questions so that the problem is clearly stated. Their ethics do not permit "trick" or "catch" questions. Questions may have been tried out on sample groups, or subjected to statistical analysis, to determine their usefulness.

Written tests are often used in combination with performance tests, ratings of training and experience, and oral interviews. All of these measures combine to form the best-known means of finding the right person for the right job.

II. HOW TO PASS THE WRITTEN TEST

A. NATURE OF THE EXAMINATION

To prepare intelligently for civil service examinations, you should know how they differ from school examinations you have taken. In school you were assigned certain definite pages to read or subjects to cover. The examination questions were quite detailed and usually emphasized memory. Civil service exams, on the other hand, try to discover your present ability to perform the duties of a position, plus your potentiality to learn these duties. In other words, a civil service exam attempts to predict how successful you will be. Questions cover such a broad area that they cannot be as minute and detailed as school exam questions.

In the public service similar kinds of work, or positions, are grouped together in one "class." This process is known as *position-classification*. All the positions in a class are paid according to the salary range for that class. One class title covers all of these positions, and they are all tested by the same examination.

B. FOUR BASIC STEPS

1) Study the announcement

How, then, can you know what subjects to study? Our best answer is: "Learn as much as possible about the class of positions for which you've applied." The exam will test the knowledge, skills and abilities needed to do the work.

Your most valuable source of information about the position you want is the official exam announcement. This announcement lists the training and experience qualifications. Check these standards and apply only if you come reasonably close to meeting them.

The brief description of the position in the examination announcement offers some clues to the subjects which will be tested. Think about the job itself. Review the duties in your mind. Can you perform them, or are there some in which you are rusty? Fill in the blank spots in your preparation.

Many jurisdictions preview the written test in the exam announcement by including a section called "Knowledge and Abilities Required," "Scope of the Examination," or some similar heading. Here you will find out specifically what fields will be tested.

2) Review your own background

Once you learn in general what the position is all about, and what you need to know to do the work, ask yourself which subjects you already know fairly well and which need improvement. You may wonder whether to concentrate on improving your strong areas or on building some background in your fields of weakness. When the announcement has specified "some knowledge" or "considerable knowledge," or has used adjectives like "beginning principles of…" or "advanced … methods," you can get a clue as to the number and difficulty of questions to be asked in any given field. More questions, and hence broader coverage, would be included for those subjects which are more important in the work. Now weigh your strengths and weaknesses against the job requirements and prepare accordingly.

3) Determine the level of the position

Another way to tell how intensively you should prepare is to understand the level of the job for which you are applying. Is it the entering level? In other words, is this the position in which beginners in a field of work are hired? Or is it an intermediate or advanced level? Sometimes this is indicated by such words as "Junior" or "Senior" in the class title. Other jurisdictions use Roman numerals to designate the level – Clerk I, Clerk II, for example. The word "Supervisor" sometimes appears in the title. If the level is not indicated by the title, check the description of duties. Will you be working under very close supervision, or will you have responsibility for independent decisions in this work?

4) Choose appropriate study materials

Now that you know the subjects to be examined and the relative amount of each subject to be covered, you can choose suitable study materials. For beginning level jobs, or even advanced ones, if you have a pronounced weakness in some aspect of your training, read a modern, standard textbook in that field. Be sure it is up to date and has general coverage. Such books are normally available at your library, and the librarian will be glad to help you locate one. For entry-level positions, questions of appropriate difficulty are chosen – neither highly advanced questions, nor those too simple. Such questions require careful thought but not advanced training.

If the position for which you are applying is technical or advanced, you will read more advanced, specialized material. If you are already familiar with the basic principles of your field, elementary textbooks would waste your time. Concentrate on advanced textbooks and technical periodicals. Think through the concepts and review difficult problems in your field.

These are all general sources. You can get more ideas on your own initiative, following these leads. For example, training manuals and publications of the government agency which employs workers in your field can be useful, particularly for technical and professional positions. A letter or visit to the government department involved may result in more specific study suggestions, and certainly will provide you with a more definite idea of the exact nature of the position you are seeking.

III. KINDS OF TESTS

Tests are used for purposes other than measuring knowledge and ability to perform specified duties. For some positions, it is equally important to test ability to make adjustments to new situations or to profit from training. In others, basic mental abilities not dependent on information are essential. Questions which test these things may not appear as pertinent to the duties of the position as those which test for knowledge and information. Yet they are often highly important parts of a fair examination. For very general questions, it is almost impossible to help you direct your study efforts. What we can do is to point out some of the more common of these general abilities needed in public service positions and describe some typical questions.

1) General information

Broad, general information has been found useful for predicting job success in some kinds of work. This is tested in a variety of ways, from vocabulary lists to questions about current events. Basic background in some field of work, such as sociology or economics, may be sampled in a group of questions. Often these are principles which have become familiar to most persons through exposure rather than through formal training. It is difficult to advise you how to study for these questions; being alert to the world around you is our best suggestion.

2) Verbal ability

An example of an ability needed in many positions is verbal or language ability. Verbal ability is, in brief, the ability to use and understand words. Vocabulary and grammar tests are typical measures of this ability. Reading comprehension or paragraph interpretation questions are common in many kinds of civil service tests. You are given a paragraph of written material and asked to find its central meaning.

3) Numerical ability

Number skills can be tested by the familiar arithmetic problem, by checking paired lists of numbers to see which are alike and which are different, or by interpreting charts and graphs. In the latter test, a graph may be printed in the test booklet which you are asked to use as the basis for answering questions.

4) Observation

A popular test for law-enforcement positions is the observation test. A picture is shown to you for several minutes, then taken away. Questions about the picture test your ability to observe both details and larger elements.

5) Following directions

In many positions in the public service, the employee must be able to carry out written instructions dependably and accurately. You may be given a chart with several columns, each column listing a variety of information. The questions require you to carry out directions involving the information given in the chart.

6) Skills and aptitudes

Performance tests effectively measure some manual skills and aptitudes. When the skill is one in which you are trained, such as typing or shorthand, you can practice. These tests are often very much like those given in business school or high school courses. For many of the other skills and aptitudes, however, no short-time preparation can be made. Skills and abilities natural to you or that you have developed throughout your lifetime are being tested.

Many of the general questions just described provide all the data needed to answer the questions and ask you to use your reasoning ability to find the answers. Your best preparation for these tests, as well as for tests of facts and ideas, is to be at your physical and mental best. You, no doubt, have your own methods of getting into an exam-taking mood and keeping "in shape." The next section lists some ideas on this subject.

IV. KINDS OF QUESTIONS

Only rarely is the "essay" question, which you answer in narrative form, used in civil service tests. Civil service tests are usually of the short-answer type. Full instructions for answering these questions will be given to you at the examination. But in case this is your first experience with short-answer questions and separate answer sheets, here is what you need to know:

1) Multiple-choice Questions

Most popular of the short-answer questions is the "multiple choice" or "best answer" question. It can be used, for example, to test for factual knowledge, ability to solve problems or judgment in meeting situations found at work.

A multiple-choice question is normally one of three types—

- It can begin with an incomplete statement followed by several possible endings. You are to find the one ending which *best* completes the statement, although some of the others may not be entirely wrong.
- It can also be a complete statement in the form of a question which is answered by choosing one of the statements listed.
- It can be in the form of a problem – again you select the best answer.

Here is an example of a multiple-choice question with a discussion which should give you some clues as to the method for choosing the right answer:

When an employee has a complaint about his assignment, the action which will *best* help him overcome his difficulty is to
  A. discuss his difficulty with his coworkers
  B. take the problem to the head of the organization
  C. take the problem to the person who gave him the assignment
  D. say nothing to anyone about his complaint

In answering this question, you should study each of the choices to find which is best. Consider choice "A" – Certainly an employee may discuss his complaint with fellow employees, but no change or improvement can result, and the complaint remains unresolved. Choice "B" is a poor choice since the head of the organization probably does not know what assignment you have been given, and taking your problem to him is known as "going over the head" of the supervisor. The supervisor, or person who made the assignment, is the person who can clarify it or correct any injustice. Choice "C" is, therefore, correct. To say nothing, as in choice "D," is unwise. Supervisors have and interest in knowing the problems employees are facing, and the employee is seeking a solution to his problem.

2) True/False Questions

The "true/false" or "right/wrong" form of question is sometimes used. Here a complete statement is given. Your job is to decide whether the statement is right or wrong.

SAMPLE: A roaming cell-phone call to a nearby city costs less than a non-roaming call to a distant city.

This statement is wrong, or false, since roaming calls are more expensive.

This is not a complete list of all possible question forms, although most of the others are variations of these common types. You will always get complete directions for answering questions. Be sure you understand *how* to mark your answers – ask questions until you do.

V. RECORDING YOUR ANSWERS

Computer terminals are used more and more today for many different kinds of exams.

For an examination with very few applicants, you may be told to record your answers in the test booklet itself. Separate answer sheets are much more common. If this separate answer sheet is to be scored by machine – and this is often the case – it is highly important that you mark your answers correctly in order to get credit.

An electronic scoring machine is often used in civil service offices because of the speed with which papers can be scored. Machine-scored answer sheets must be marked with a pencil, which will be given to you. This pencil has a high graphite content which responds to the electronic scoring machine. As a matter of fact, stray dots may register as answers, so do not let your pencil rest on the answer sheet while you are pondering the correct answer. Also, if your pencil lead breaks or is otherwise defective, ask for another.

Since the answer sheet will be dropped in a slot in the scoring machine, be careful not to bend the corners or get the paper crumpled.

The answer sheet normally has five vertical columns of numbers, with 30 numbers to a column. These numbers correspond to the question numbers in your test booklet. After each number, going across the page are four or five pairs of dotted lines. These short dotted lines have small letters or numbers above them. The first two pairs may also have a "T" or "F" above the letters. This indicates that the first two pairs only are to be used if the questions are of the true-false type. If the questions are multiple choice, disregard the "T" and "F" and pay attention only to the small letters or numbers.

Answer your questions in the manner of the sample that follows:

32. The largest city in the United States is
    A. Washington, D.C.
    B. New York City
    C. Chicago
    D. Detroit
    E. San Francisco

1) Choose the answer you think is best. (New York City is the largest, so "B" is correct.)
2) Find the row of dotted lines numbered the same as the question you are answering. (Find row number 32)
3) Find the pair of dotted lines corresponding to the answer. (Find the pair of lines under the mark "B.")
4) Make a solid black mark between the dotted lines.

VI. BEFORE THE TEST

Common sense will help you find procedures to follow to get ready for an examination. Too many of us, however, overlook these sensible measures. Indeed, nervousness and fatigue have been found to be the most serious reasons why applicants fail to do their best on civil service tests. Here is a list of reminders:

- Begin your preparation early – Don't wait until the last minute to go scurrying around for books and materials or to find out what the position is all about.
- Prepare continuously – An hour a night for a week is better than an all-night cram session. This has been definitely established. What is more, a night a week for a month will return better dividends than crowding your study into a shorter period of time.
- Locate the place of the exam – You have been sent a notice telling you when and where to report for the examination. If the location is in a different town or otherwise unfamiliar to you, it would be well to inquire the best route and learn something about the building.
- Relax the night before the test – Allow your mind to rest. Do not study at all that night. Plan some mild recreation or diversion; then go to bed early and get a good night's sleep.
- Get up early enough to make a leisurely trip to the place for the test – This way unforeseen events, traffic snarls, unfamiliar buildings, etc. will not upset you.
- Dress comfortably – A written test is not a fashion show. You will be known by number and not by name, so wear something comfortable.
- Leave excess paraphernalia at home – Shopping bags and odd bundles will get in your way. You need bring only the items mentioned in the official notice you received; usually everything you need is provided. Do not bring reference books to the exam. They will only confuse those last minutes and be taken away from you when in the test room.
- Arrive somewhat ahead of time – If because of transportation schedules you must get there very early, bring a newspaper or magazine to take your mind off yourself while waiting.
- Locate the examination room – When you have found the proper room, you will be directed to the seat or part of the room where you will sit. Sometimes you are given a sheet of instructions to read while you are waiting. Do not fill out any forms until you are told to do so; just read them and be prepared.
- Relax and prepare to listen to the instructions
- If you have any physical problem that may keep you from doing your best, be sure to tell the test administrator. If you are sick or in poor health, you really cannot do your best on the exam. You can come back and take the test some other time.

VII. AT THE TEST

The day of the test is here and you have the test booklet in your hand. The temptation to get going is very strong. Caution! There is more to success than knowing the right answers. You must know how to identify your papers and understand variations in the type of short-answer question used in this particular examination. Follow these suggestions for maximum results from your efforts:

1) Cooperate with the monitor

The test administrator has a duty to create a situation in which you can be as much at ease as possible. He will give instructions, tell you when to begin, check to see that you are marking your answer sheet correctly, and so on. He is not there to guard you, although he will see that your competitors do not take unfair advantage. He wants to help you do your best.

2) Listen to all instructions

Don't jump the gun! Wait until you understand all directions. In most civil service tests you get more time than you need to answer the questions. So don't be in a hurry. Read each word of instructions until you clearly understand the meaning. Study the examples, listen to all announcements and follow directions. Ask questions if you do not understand what to do.

3) Identify your papers

Civil service exams are usually identified by number only. You will be assigned a number; you must not put your name on your test papers. Be sure to copy your number correctly. Since more than one exam may be given, copy your exact examination title.

4) Plan your time

Unless you are told that a test is a "speed" or "rate of work" test, speed itself is usually not important. Time enough to answer all the questions will be provided, but this does not mean that you have all day. An overall time limit has been set. Divide the total time (in minutes) by the number of questions to determine the approximate time you have for each question.

5) Do not linger over difficult questions

If you come across a difficult question, mark it with a paper clip (useful to have along) and come back to it when you have been through the booklet. One caution if you do this – be sure to skip a number on your answer sheet as well. Check often to be sure that you have not lost your place and that you are marking in the row numbered the same as the question you are answering.

6) Read the questions

Be sure you know what the question asks! Many capable people are unsuccessful because they failed to *read* the questions correctly.

7) Answer all questions

Unless you have been instructed that a penalty will be deducted for incorrect answers, it is better to guess than to omit a question.

8) Speed tests

It is often better NOT to guess on speed tests. It has been found that on timed tests people are tempted to spend the last few seconds before time is called in marking answers at random – without even reading them – in the hope of picking up a few extra points. To discourage this practice, the instructions may warn you that your score will be "corrected" for guessing. That is, a penalty will be applied. The incorrect answers will be deducted from the correct ones, or some other penalty formula will be used.

9) Review your answers

If you finish before time is called, go back to the questions you guessed or omitted to give them further thought. Review other answers if you have time.

10) Return your test materials

If you are ready to leave before others have finished or time is called, take ALL your materials to the monitor and leave quietly. Never take any test material with you. The monitor can discover whose papers are not complete, and taking a test booklet may be grounds for disqualification.

VIII. EXAMINATION TECHNIQUES

1) Read the general instructions carefully. These are usually printed on the first page of the exam booklet. As a rule, these instructions refer to the timing of the examination; the fact that you should not start work until the signal and must stop work at a signal, etc. If there are any *special* instructions, such as a choice of questions to be answered, make sure that you note this instruction carefully.

2) When you are ready to start work on the examination, that is as soon as the signal has been given, read the instructions to each question booklet, underline any key words or phrases, such as *least, best, outline, describe* and the like. In this way you will tend to answer as requested rather than discover on reviewing your paper that you *listed without describing*, that you selected the *worst* choice rather than the *best* choice, etc.

3) If the examination is of the objective or multiple-choice type – that is, each question will also give a series of possible answers: A, B, C or D, and you are called upon to select the best answer and write the letter next to that answer on your answer paper – it is advisable to start answering each question in turn. There may be anywhere from 50 to 100 such questions in the three or four hours allotted and you can see how much time would be taken if you read through all the questions before beginning to answer any. Furthermore, if you come across a question or group of questions which you know would be difficult to answer, it would undoubtedly affect your handling of all the other questions.

4) If the examination is of the essay type and contains but a few questions, it is a moot point as to whether you should read all the questions before starting to answer any one. Of course, if you are given a choice – say five out of seven and the like – then it is essential to read all the questions so you can eliminate the two that are most difficult. If, however, you are asked to answer all the questions, there may be danger in trying to answer the easiest one first because you may find that you will spend too much time on it. The best technique is to answer the first question, then proceed to the second, etc.

5) Time your answers. Before the exam begins, write down the time it started, then add the time allowed for the examination and write down the time it must be completed, then divide the time available somewhat as follows:

- If 3-1/2 hours are allowed, that would be 210 minutes. If you have 80 objective-type questions, that would be an average of 2-1/2 minutes per question. Allow yourself no more than 2 minutes per question, or a total of 160 minutes, which will permit about 50 minutes to review.
- If for the time allotment of 210 minutes there are 7 essay questions to answer, that would average about 30 minutes a question. Give yourself only 25 minutes per question so that you have about 35 minutes to review.

6) The most important instruction is to *read each question* and make sure you know what is wanted. The second most important instruction is to *time yourself properly* so that you answer every question. The third most important instruction is to *answer every question*. Guess if you have to but include something for each question. Remember that you will receive no credit for a blank and will probably receive some credit if you write something in answer to an essay question. If you guess a letter – say "B" for a multiple-choice question – you may have guessed right. If you leave a blank as an answer to a multiple-choice question, the examiners may respect your feelings but it will not add a point to your score. Some exams may penalize you for wrong answers, so in such cases *only*, you may not want to guess unless you have some basis for your answer.

7) Suggestions
   a. Objective-type questions
      1. Examine the question booklet for proper sequence of pages and questions
      2. Read all instructions carefully
      3. Skip any question which seems too difficult; return to it after all other questions have been answered
      4. Apportion your time properly; do not spend too much time on any single question or group of questions
      5. Note and underline key words – *all, most, fewest, least, best, worst, same, opposite,* etc.
      6. Pay particular attention to negatives
      7. Note unusual option, e.g., unduly long, short, complex, different or similar in content to the body of the question
      8. Observe the use of "hedging" words – *probably, may, most likely,* etc.
      9. Make sure that your answer is put next to the same number as the question
      10. Do not second-guess unless you have good reason to believe the second answer is definitely more correct
      11. Cross out original answer if you decide another answer is more accurate; do not erase until you are ready to hand your paper in
      12. Answer all questions; guess unless instructed otherwise
      13. Leave time for review

   b. Essay questions
      1. Read each question carefully
      2. Determine exactly what is wanted. Underline key words or phrases.
      3. Decide on outline or paragraph answer

4. Include many different points and elements unless asked to develop any one or two points or elements
5. Show impartiality by giving pros and cons unless directed to select one side only
6. Make and write down any assumptions you find necessary to answer the questions
7. Watch your English, grammar, punctuation and choice of words
8. Time your answers; don't crowd material

8) Answering the essay question

Most essay questions can be answered by framing the specific response around several key words or ideas. Here are a few such key words or ideas:

M's: manpower, materials, methods, money, management
P's: purpose, program, policy, plan, procedure, practice, problems, pitfalls, personnel, public relations
   a. Six basic steps in handling problems:
      1. Preliminary plan and background development
      2. Collect information, data and facts
      3. Analyze and interpret information, data and facts
      4. Analyze and develop solutions as well as make recommendations
      5. Prepare report and sell recommendations
      6. Install recommendations and follow up effectiveness

   b. Pitfalls to avoid
      1. *Taking things for granted* – A statement of the situation does not necessarily imply that each of the elements is necessarily true; for example, a complaint may be invalid and biased so that all that can be taken for granted is that a complaint has been registered
      2. *Considering only one side of a situation* – Wherever possible, indicate several alternatives and then point out the reasons you selected the best one
      3. *Failing to indicate follow up* – Whenever your answer indicates action on your part, make certain that you will take proper follow-up action to see how successful your recommendations, procedures or actions turn out to be
      4. *Taking too long in answering any single question* – Remember to time your answers properly

IX. AFTER THE TEST

Scoring procedures differ in detail among civil service jurisdictions although the general principles are the same. Whether the papers are hand-scored or graded by machine we have described, they are nearly always graded by number. That is, the person who marks the paper knows only the number – never the name – of the applicant. Not until all the papers have been graded will they be matched with names. If other tests, such as training and experience or oral interview ratings have been given, scores will be combined. Different parts of the examination usually have different weights. For example, the written test might count 60 percent of the final grade, and a rating of training and experience 40 percent. In many jurisdictions, veterans will have a certain number of points added to their grades.

After the final grade has been determined, the names are placed in grade order and an eligible list is established. There are various methods for resolving ties between those who get the same final grade – probably the most common is to place first the name of the person whose application was received first. Job offers are made from the eligible list in the order the names appear on it. You will be notified of your grade and your rank as soon as all these computations have been made. This will be done as rapidly as possible.

People who are found to meet the requirements in the announcement are called "eligibles." Their names are put on a list of eligible candidates. An eligible's chances of getting a job depend on how high he stands on this list and how fast agencies are filling jobs from the list.

When a job is to be filled from a list of eligibles, the agency asks for the names of people on the list of eligibles for that job. When the civil service commission receives this request, it sends to the agency the names of the three people highest on this list. Or, if the job to be filled has specialized requirements, the office sends the agency the names of the top three persons who meet these requirements from the general list.

The appointing officer makes a choice from among the three people whose names were sent to him. If the selected person accepts the appointment, the names of the others are put back on the list to be considered for future openings.

That is the rule in hiring from all kinds of eligible lists, whether they are for typist, carpenter, chemist, or something else. For every vacancy, the appointing officer has his choice of any one of the top three eligibles on the list. This explains why the person whose name is on top of the list sometimes does not get an appointment when some of the persons lower on the list do. If the appointing officer chooses the second or third eligible, the No. 1 eligible does not get a job at once, but stays on the list until he is appointed or the list is terminated.

X. HOW TO PASS THE INTERVIEW TEST

The examination for which you applied requires an oral interview test. You have already taken the written test and you are now being called for the interview test – the final part of the formal examination.

You may think that it is not possible to prepare for an interview test and that there are no procedures to follow during an interview. Our purpose is to point out some things you can do in advance that will help you and some good rules to follow and pitfalls to avoid while you are being interviewed.

What is an interview supposed to test?

The written examination is designed to test the technical knowledge and competence of the candidate; the oral is designed to evaluate intangible qualities, not readily measured otherwise, and to establish a list showing the relative fitness of each candidate – as measured against his competitors – for the position sought. Scoring is not on the basis of "right" and "wrong," but on a sliding scale of values ranging from "not passable" to "outstanding." As a matter of fact, it is possible to achieve a relatively low score without a single "incorrect" answer because of evident weakness in the qualities being measured.

Occasionally, an examination may consist entirely of an oral test – either an individual or a group oral. In such cases, information is sought concerning the technical knowledges and abilities of the candidate, since there has been no written examination for this purpose. More commonly, however, an oral test is used to supplement a written examination.

Who conducts interviews?

The composition of oral boards varies among different jurisdictions. In nearly all, a representative of the personnel department serves as chairman. One of the members of the board may be a representative of the department in which the candidate would work. In some cases, "outside experts" are used, and, frequently, a businessman or some other representative of the general public is asked to serve. Labor and management or other special groups may be represented. The aim is to secure the services of experts in the appropriate field.

However the board is composed, it is a good idea (and not at all improper or unethical) to ascertain in advance of the interview who the members are and what groups they represent. When you are introduced to them, you will have some idea of their backgrounds and interests, and at least you will not stutter and stammer over their names.

What should be done before the interview?

While knowledge about the board members is useful and takes some of the surprise element out of the interview, there is other preparation which is more substantive. It *is* possible to prepare for an oral interview – in several ways:

1) Keep a copy of your application and review it carefully before the interview

This may be the only document before the oral board, and the starting point of the interview. Know what education and experience you have listed there, and the sequence and dates of all of it. Sometimes the board will ask you to review the highlights of your experience for them; you should not have to hem and haw doing it.

2) Study the class specification and the examination announcement

Usually, the oral board has one or both of these to guide them. The qualities, characteristics or knowledges required by the position sought are stated in these documents. They offer valuable clues as to the nature of the oral interview. For example, if the job involves supervisory responsibilities, the announcement will usually indicate that knowledge of modern supervisory methods and the qualifications of the candidate as a supervisor will be tested. If so, you can expect such questions, frequently in the form of a hypothetical situation which you are expected to solve. NEVER go into an oral without knowledge of the duties and responsibilities of the job you seek.

3) Think through each qualification required

Try to visualize the kind of questions you would ask if you were a board member. How well could you answer them? Try especially to appraise your own knowledge and background in each area, *measured against the job sought*, and identify any areas in which you are weak. Be critical and realistic – do not flatter yourself.

4) Do some general reading in areas in which you feel you may be weak

For example, if the job involves supervision and your past experience has NOT, some general reading in supervisory methods and practices, particularly in the field of human relations, might be useful. Do NOT study agency procedures or detailed manuals. The oral board will be testing your understanding and capacity, not your memory.

5) Get a good night's sleep and watch your general health and mental attitude

You will want a clear head at the interview. Take care of a cold or any other minor ailment, and of course, no hangovers.

What should be done on the day of the interview?

Now comes the day of the interview itself. Give yourself plenty of time to get there. Plan to arrive somewhat ahead of the scheduled time, particularly if your appointment is in the fore part of the day. If a previous candidate fails to appear, the board might be ready for you a bit early. By early afternoon an oral board is almost invariably behind schedule if there are many candidates, and you may have to wait. Take along a book or magazine to read, or your application to review, but leave any extraneous material in the waiting room when you go in for your interview. In any event, relax and compose yourself.

The matter of dress is important. The board is forming impressions about you – from your experience, your manners, your attitude, and your appearance. Give your personal appearance careful attention. Dress your best, but not your flashiest. Choose conservative, appropriate clothing, and be sure it is immaculate. This is a business interview, and your appearance should indicate that you regard it as such. Besides, being well groomed and properly dressed will help boost your confidence.

Sooner or later, someone will call your name and escort you into the interview room. *This is it.* From here on you are on your own. It is too late for any more preparation. But remember, you asked for this opportunity to prove your fitness, and you are here because your request was granted.

What happens when you go in?

The usual sequence of events will be as follows: The clerk (who is often the board stenographer) will introduce you to the chairman of the oral board, who will introduce you to the other members of the board. Acknowledge the introductions before you sit down. Do not be surprised if you find a microphone facing you or a stenotypist sitting by. Oral interviews are usually recorded in the event of an appeal or other review.

Usually the chairman of the board will open the interview by reviewing the highlights of your education and work experience from your application – primarily for the benefit of the other members of the board, as well as to get the material into the record. Do not interrupt or comment unless there is an error or significant misinterpretation; if that is the case, do not hesitate. But do not quibble about insignificant matters. Also, he will usually ask you some question about your education, experience or your present job – partly to get you to start talking and to establish the interviewing "rapport." He may start the actual questioning, or turn it over to one of the other members. Frequently, each member undertakes the questioning on a particular area, one in which he is perhaps most competent, so you can expect each member to participate in the examination. Because time is limited, you may also expect some rather abrupt switches in the direction the questioning takes, so do not be upset by it. Normally, a board member will not pursue a single line of questioning unless he discovers a particular strength or weakness.

After each member has participated, the chairman will usually ask whether any member has any further questions, then will ask you if you have anything you wish to add. Unless you are expecting this question, it may floor you. Worse, it may start you off on an extended, extemporaneous speech. The board is not usually seeking more information. The question is principally to offer you a last opportunity to present further qualifications or to indicate that you have nothing to add. So, if you feel that a significant qualification or characteristic has been overlooked, it is proper to point it out in a sentence or so. Do not compliment the board on the thoroughness of their examination – they have been sketchy, and you know it. If you wish, merely say, "No thank you, I have nothing further to add." This is a point where you can "talk yourself out" of a good impression or fail to present an important bit of information. Remember, *you close the interview yourself.*

The chairman will then say, "That is all, Mr. _____, thank you." Do not be startled; the interview is over, and quicker than you think. Thank him, gather your belongings and take your leave. Save your sigh of relief for the other side of the door.

How to put your best foot forward

Throughout this entire process, you may feel that the board individually and collectively is trying to pierce your defenses, seek out your hidden weaknesses and embarrass and confuse you. Actually, this is not true. They are obliged to make an appraisal of your qualifications for the job you are seeking, and they want to see you in your best light. Remember, they must interview all candidates and a non-cooperative candidate may become a failure in spite of their best efforts to bring out his qualifications. Here are 15 suggestions that will help you:

1) Be natural – Keep your attitude confident, not cocky

If you are not confident that you can do the job, do not expect the board to be. Do not apologize for your weaknesses, try to bring out your strong points. The board is interested in a positive, not negative, presentation. Cockiness will antagonize any board member and make him wonder if you are covering up a weakness by a false show of strength.

2) Get comfortable, but don't lounge or sprawl

Sit erectly but not stiffly. A careless posture may lead the board to conclude that you are careless in other things, or at least that you are not impressed by the importance of the occasion. Either conclusion is natural, even if incorrect. Do not fuss with your clothing, a pencil or an ashtray. Your hands may occasionally be useful to emphasize a point; do not let them become a point of distraction.

3) Do not wisecrack or make small talk

This is a serious situation, and your attitude should show that you consider it as such. Further, the time of the board is limited – they do not want to waste it, and neither should you.

4) Do not exaggerate your experience or abilities

In the first place, from information in the application or other interviews and sources, the board may know more about you than you think. Secondly, you probably will not get away with it. An experienced board is rather adept at spotting such a situation, so do not take the chance.

5) If you know a board member, do not make a point of it, yet do not hide it

Certainly you are not fooling him, and probably not the other members of the board. Do not try to take advantage of your acquaintanceship – it will probably do you little good.

6) Do not dominate the interview

Let the board do that. They will give you the clues – do not assume that you have to do all the talking. Realize that the board has a number of questions to ask you, and do not try to take up all the interview time by showing off your extensive knowledge of the answer to the first one.

7) Be attentive

You only have 20 minutes or so, and you should keep your attention at its sharpest throughout. When a member is addressing a problem or question to you, give him your undivided attention. Address your reply principally to him, but do not exclude the other board members.

8) Do not interrupt

A board member may be stating a problem for you to analyze. He will ask you a question when the time comes. Let him state the problem, and wait for the question.

9) Make sure you understand the question

Do not try to answer until you are sure what the question is. If it is not clear, restate it in your own words or ask the board member to clarify it for you. However, do not haggle about minor elements.

10) Reply promptly but not hastily

A common entry on oral board rating sheets is "candidate responded readily," or "candidate hesitated in replies." Respond as promptly and quickly as you can, but do not jump to a hasty, ill-considered answer.

11) Do not be peremptory in your answers

A brief answer is proper – but do not fire your answer back. That is a losing game from your point of view. The board member can probably ask questions much faster than you can answer them.

12) Do not try to create the answer you think the board member wants

He is interested in what kind of mind you have and how it works – not in playing games. Furthermore, he can usually spot this practice and will actually grade you down on it.

13) Do not switch sides in your reply merely to agree with a board member

Frequently, a member will take a contrary position merely to draw you out and to see if you are willing and able to defend your point of view. Do not start a debate, yet do not surrender a good position. If a position is worth taking, it is worth defending.

14) Do not be afraid to admit an error in judgment if you are shown to be wrong

The board knows that you are forced to reply without any opportunity for careful consideration. Your answer may be demonstrably wrong. If so, admit it and get on with the interview.

15) Do not dwell at length on your present job

The opening question may relate to your present assignment. Answer the question but do not go into an extended discussion. You are being examined for a *new* job, not your present one. As a matter of fact, try to phrase ALL your answers in terms of the job for which you are being examined.

Basis of Rating

Probably you will forget most of these "do's" and "don'ts" when you walk into the oral interview room. Even remembering them all will not ensure you a passing grade. Perhaps you did not have the qualifications in the first place. But remembering them will help you to put your best foot forward, without treading on the toes of the board members.

Rumor and popular opinion to the contrary notwithstanding, an oral board wants you to make the best appearance possible. They know you are under pressure – but they also want to see how you respond to it as a guide to what your reaction would be under the pressures of the job you seek. They will be influenced by the degree of poise you display, the personal traits you show and the manner in which you respond.

ABOUT THIS BOOK

This book contains tests divided into Examination Sections. Go through each test, answering every question in the margin. At the end of each test look at the answer key and check your answers. On the ones you got wrong, look at the right answer choice and learn. Do not fill in the answers first. Do not memorize the questions and answers, but understand the answer and principles involved. On your test, the questions will likely be different from the samples. Questions are changed and new ones added. If you understand these past questions you should have success with any changes that arise. Tests may consist of several types of questions. We have additional books on each subject should more study be advisable or necessary for you. Finally, the more you study, the better prepared you will be. This book is intended to be the last thing you study before you walk into the examination room. Prior study of relevant texts is also recommended. NLC publishes some of these in our Fundamental Series. Knowledge and good sense are important factors in passing your exam. Good luck also helps. So now study this Passbook, absorb the material contained within and take that knowledge into the examination. Then do your best to pass that exam.

EXAMINATION SECTION

EXAMINATION SECTION

TEST 1

DIRECTIONS: Each question or incomplete statement is followed by several suggested answers or completions. Select the one that BEST answers the question or completes the statement. *PRINT THE LETTER OF THE CORRECT ANSWER IN THE SPACE AT THE RIGHT.*

1. What is the default compressing software of Windows?   1.____
   A. WinRar   B. 7-zip
   C. WinZip   D. All of the above

2. Which software does NOT require special drives to run?   2.____
   A. Mouse   B. Keyboard
   C. Joystick   D. All of the above

3. What software is required to run PDF?   3.____
   A. MS Word   B. Windows Media Player
   C. Adobe Photoshop   D. Adobe Reader

4. An error message that says "there is a problem with this website's security certificate" appears when   4.____
   A. Windows is outdated   B. browser is outdated
   C. date and time are wrong D. internet is disabled

5. Software should always be _____ for better performance.   5.____
   A. disabled   B. updated
   C. uninstalled   D. all of the above

6. SATA is the abbreviation for   6.____
   A. Sequential Advanced Technology Advancement
   B. Serial Advanced Technology Attachment
   C. Serial Automatic Technology Attachment
   D. Supper Advanced Technology Attachment

7. Which of the following is a part of management software development?   7.____
   A. People   B. Product
   C. Process   D. All of the above

8. _____ is a tool in the design phase.   8.____
   A. Abstraction   B. Refinement
   C. Information Hiding   D. All of the above

9. What is the other name used for white box software testing technique?   9.____
   A. Basic Path   B. Graph Testing
   C. Data Flow   D. Glass Box Testing

1

10. _____ is included in the Turnkey package.   10.____
    A. Software   B. Hardware
    C. Training   D. All of the above

11. _____ are types of a record access method.   11.____
    A. Sequential and random   B. Direct and immediate
    C. Sequential and indexed   D. Online and real time

12. _____ has a sequential file organization.   12.____
    A. Grocery store checkout   B. Bank checking account
    C. Payroll   D. Airline reservation

13. What will you recommend when users are involved in complex tasks?   13.____
    A. A short term memory   B. Demands on shortcut usage
    C. Both A and B   D. None of the above

14. _____ protocols are similar to HTTP.   14.____
    A. FTP; SMTP   B. FTP; SNMP
    C. FTP; MTV   D. SMTP; SNMP

15. _____ is the oldest data model.   15.____
    A. Relational   B. Deductive
    C. Physical   D. Hierarchical

16. _____ defines the transaction executed.   16.____
    A. Committed   B. Aborted
    C. Failed   D. Rolled Back

17. _____ is NOT a deadlock managing strategy.   17.____
    A. Deadlock prevention   B. Timeout
    C. Deadlock detection   D. Deadlock annihilation

18. _____ is the average execution time of the monitor power process. 18.____
    A. 1 ms   B. 10 ms
    C. 100 ms   D. None of the above

19. _____ is NOT a dimension of scalability.   19.____
    A. Size   B. Distribution
    C. Interception   D. Manageability

20. What would you do if the icons on the desktop are white or missing colors?   20.____
    A. End the explorer.exe   B. Check settings in Appearance
    C. Both A and B   D. None of the above

21. What would you do if while using AutoCAD you receive a message of "license   21.____
is invalid"?
    A. Delete licensing file   B. Re-enter registration information
    C. Both A and B   D. None of the above

22. What would you do to satisfy the growing communication need in your company?
    A. Use front end processor   B. Use a multiplexer
    C. Use a controller   D. All of the above

22.____

23. _____ is a part of x.25.
    A. Technique for start stop data   B. Technique for dial access
    C. DTE/DCE interface   D. None of the above

23.____

24. Which of the following is a software product?
    A. CAD, Cam   B. Firmware, Embedded
    C. Generic, Customized   D. Both A and B

24.____

25. ACT in Boehm software maintenance model is the abbreviation for
    A. Actual Change Track   B. Annual Change Track
    C. Annual Change Traffic   D. Actual Change Traffic

25.____

KEY (CORRECT ANSWERS)

1.	C		11.	A
2.	D		12.	B
3.	D		13.	A
4.	C		14.	A
5.	B		15.	D
6.	B		16.	A
7.	D		17.	D
8.	D		18.	A
9.	D		19.	D
10.	D		20.	C

21.	C
22.	D
23.	C
24.	C
25.	C

TEST 2

DIRECTIONS: Each question or incomplete statement is followed by several suggested answers or completions. Select the one that BEST answers the question or completes the statement. *PRINT THE LETTER OF THE CORRECT ANSWER IN THE SPACE AT THE RIGHT.*

1. Software maintenance incorporates
   A. Error Correction
   B. Enhancement of capabilities
   C. Deletion of obsolete capabilities
   D. All of the above

   1.____

2. Software Maintenance model called Taute has _____ number of phases.
   A. 6   B. 7   C. 8   D. 9

   2.____

3. _____ is a software process certification.
   A. JAVA certified
   B. IBM certified
   C. ISO-9000
   D. Microsoft certified

   3.____

4. _____ is known as quality management in software development.
   A. SQA
   B. SQM
   C. SQI
   D. Both A and B

   4.____

5. Software reliability means
   A. time   B. efficiency   C. quality   D. speed

   5.____

6. A software package designed to store and manage databases is
   A. Database   B. DBMS   C. Data Model   D. Data

   6.____

7.

   The above image represents a _____ relation.
   A. many to many
   B. many to one
   C. one to one
   D. one to many

   7.____

8. The diagram shown at the right indicates that
   A. there is a missing entity
   B. students attend courses
   C. many students can attend many courses
   D. students have to attend more than one course

   8.____

9. In relational algebra, the union of two sets (set A and set B) corresponds to
   A. A OR B   B. A + B   C. A AND B   D. A - B

   9.____

10. _____ is the location of the keyboard status byte.
    A. 0040:0000H   B. 0040:0013H
    C. 0040:0015H   D. 0040:0017H

10.____

11. What is the number of maximum interrupts occurring in a PC?
    A. 64   B. 128   C. 256   D. 512

11.____

12. How many bytes are there in an operating system name in the boot block?
    A. 3   B. 5   C. 8   D. 11

12.____

13. What is the size of a DPB structure?
    A. 16   B. 32   C. 64   D. 128

13.____

14. _____ is the file system in CD.
    A. Contiguous   B. Chained   C. Indexed   D. None

14.____

15. NTFS volume is accessed directly in
    A. DOS   B. Linux   C. Windows   D. MAC

15.____

16. _____.com is an MS DOS file in the boot disk.
    A. Command   B. Start   C. Tree   D. Ver

16.____

17. _____ is a table in the OS that keeps information of files.
    A. FFT   B. FIT   C. FAT   D. DIT

17.____

18. _____ is a system programming language.
    A. C   B. PL/360
    C. PASCAL   D. All of the above

18.____

19. What would you do if the icons disappear from the Taskbar?
    A. Press Windows Key + R and type "regedit"
    B. Delete Icon stream and past icon Stream values
    C. Uncheck user interface
    D. All of the above

19.____

20. What would you do if you want to make sure the drivers of the old printers are removed?
    A. Check Server Properties   B. Check settings in Appearance
    C. Both A and B   D. None of the above

20.____

21. Microsoft has introduced _____ tool that incorporates all the automated fixes.
    A. Fix It Center   B. Fix All
    C. Fixing It   D. none of the above

21.____

22. A PC can only use one _____ device at a time.
    A. Ready Boost   B. Built-in Flash
    C. RAM   D. all of the above

22.____

23. You need to edit two registry keys called _____ if you cannot customize folders.
    A. bagMRU and Bags   B. RAM and ROM
    C. DTE/DCE interface   D. none of the above
      23.____

24. What would you do if your PC does not have a Windows Installation disk?
    A. Select "create a system repair" disc
    B. Place a DVD in the writeable drive
    C. Create a bootable disc by the "Repair Your Computer"
    D. All of the above
      24.____

25. Code of conduct defines the
    A. employees' legal and ethical obligations
    B. commitment to integrity
    C. terms and condition of the company
    D. legal contract
      25.____

KEY (CORRECT ANSWERS)

1.	D		11.	C
2.	C		12.	C
3.	C		13.	B
4.	A		14.	A
5.	A		15.	A
6.	B		16.	A
7.	D		17.	A
8.	C		18.	D
9.	B		19.	D
10.	D		20.	C

21.	A
22.	A
23.	A
24.	D
25.	A

TEST 3

DIRECTIONS: Each question or incomplete statement is followed by several suggested answers or completions. Select the one that BEST answers the question or completes the statement. *PRINT THE LETTER OF THE CORRECT ANSWER IN THE SPACE AT THE RIGHT.*

1. What would you do if the drive does not open by double-clicking? 1.____
   A. Check search option in drive C
   B. Enter regsvr32/l shell32.dll in the Run
   C. Check settings in the control panel
   D. Both A and B

2. What would you do if you attach another display unit to your PC but it remains blank? 2.____
   A. Check the cables
   B. Check display properties
   C. Select the properties to duplicate each other
   D. All of the above

3. _____ helps you when you are locked out of Manager and Registry Editor? 3.____
   A. Virus Effect Remover   B. Fix It Tool
   C. Safe mode   D. All of the above

4. The two types of cache memory in RAM are called 4.____
   A. ALU and CPU   B. Buffer and Procedure
   C. Date and Timing   D. DLL and STAT

5. _____ points at the same location when the keyboard buffer is empty. 5.____
   A. Interrupt   B. Head and Tail
   C. Tail   D. All of the above

6. _____ frequency is divided by the interval time. 6.____
   A. Output   B. Input
   C. Both A and B   D. None of the above
   E. All of the above

7. What is the number of PPI present in a standard PC? 7.____
   A. 1   B. 4   C. 8   D. 16

8. _____ is used as a status port of the keyboard. 8.____
   A. 64H   B. 44H
   C. 77H   D. All of the above

9. _____ is a computer with an 80286 microprocessor. 9.____
   A. XT computer   B. PC/AT computer
   C. PS/2 computer   D. None of the above

10. _____ is not a process.
    A. Arranging   B. Manipulation
    C. Calculating   D. Gathering

10._____

11. _____ is a sequential processing application.
    A. Grades processing   B. Payroll processing
    C. Both A and B   D. All of the above

11._____

12. _____ has a record disk address.
    A. Track Number   B. Sector Number
    C. Surface Number   D. All of the above

12._____

13. Which printer would you NOT use while printing on a carbon form?
    A. Daisy Wheel   B. Dot Matrix
    C. Laser   D. None of the above

13._____

14. A(n) _____ produces the BEST quality graphic production.
    A. laser printer   B. inkjet printer
    C. plotter   D. dot matrix

14._____

15. _____ allows both read and write operations at the same time.
    A. ROM   B. RAM
    C. EPROM   D. None of the above

15._____

16. _____ has the shortest access time.
    A. Cache Memory   B. Magnetic Bubble Memory
    C. Magnetic Core Memory   D. RAM

16._____

17. _____ defines the status of resources assigned to the process.
    A. Process Control   B. ALU
    C. Register Unit   D. Process Description

17._____

18. Memory _____ controls access to the memory.
    A. map   B. protection
    C. management   D. instruction

18._____

19. _____ is able to record and track all the information in a database about animal movement once placed on the animal.
    A. POS   B. RFID   C. PPS   D. GPS

19._____

20. The print of a picture taken from a digital camera is said to be a(n)
    A. data   B. output
    C. input   D. none of the above

20._____

21. _____ are the two types of record access methods.
    A. Sequential and Random   B. Direct and Immediate
    C. Online and Real Time   D. None of the above

21._____

22. _____ is the most efficient method of file organization when the file is highly active.

    A. ISAM   B. VSAM

    C. B-Tree   D. All of the above

22.____

23. _____ is the standard approach for storing data.

    A. MIS   B. Structured Programming

    C. CODASYL specification   D. None of the above

23.____

24. Which of the following RDBMS supports client server application development?

    A. dBase V   B. Oracle 7.1

    C. FoxPro 2.1   D. Both A and B

24.____

25. Which of the following techniques would you use to find the location of the element?

    A. Traversal   B. Search

    C. Sort   D. None of the above

25.____

KEY (CORRECT ANSWERS)

1.	D		11.	C
2.	D		12.	D
3.	A		13.	C
4.	B		14.	C
5.	B		15.	B
6.	B		16.	A
7.	B		17.	D
8.	A		18.	A
9.	B		19.	B
10.	D		20.	B

21.	A
22.	A
23.	C
24.	B
25.	B

TEST 4

DIRECTIONS: Each question or incomplete statement is followed by several suggested answers or completions. Select the one that BEST answers the question or completes the statement. *PRINT THE LETTER OF THE CORRECT ANSWER IN THE SPACE AT THE RIGHT.*

1. A band is equal to
   - A. a byte
   - B. a bit
   - C. 100 bits
   - D. none of the above

   1._____

2. The number of zeroes in each symbol in an odd-parity is
   - A. odd
   - B. even
   - D. unknown
   - D. both A and B

   2._____

3. _____ is also called an IPng.
   - A. IPv4
   - B. IPv5
   - C. IPv6
   - D. All of the above

   3._____

4. IPv6 addresses are written in
   - A. hexadecimal
   - B. binary
   - C. decimal
   - D. none of the above

   4._____

5. Green PCs are designed to
   - A. minimize power consumption
   - B. minimize inactive components
   - C. minimize electricity bill
   - D. all of the above

   5._____

6. Hyper V Network Virtualizations do not have the ability to access the outside world unless you
   - A. implement a forwarding agent
   - B. implement a gateway
   - C. implement a CISCO NEXUS
   - D. None of the above
   - E. All of the above

   6._____

7. What would you do to create a shortcut of a website on the desktop?
   - A. Left click on the icon present on the left side of the address bar and drag it to the desktop
   - B. Save the webpage through the Save Page As
   - C. Bookmark the page
   - D. All of the above

   7._____

8. E-mail, word documents, web pages, video and photos are called unstructured data because
   - A. they consist of text and multimedia
   - B. the data cannot be stored in a database
   - C. they cannot be stored in row and columns
   - D. all of the above

   8._____

9. What would you do to manage corporate unstructured data?   9.____
   A. Install big data tool software
   B. Install data integration tools
   C. Install business intelligence software
   D. All of the above

10. Software-defined data center is a concept for   10.____
   A. a virtualized infrastructure
   B. fully automated control of data
   C. hardware maintenance through intelligent software
   D. all of the above

11. What is a cloud database?   11.____
   A. Internet based database provided through cloud data server
   B. Database-as-a-Service
   C. Both A and B
   D. None of the above

12. Monitor footprint refers to the   12.____
   A. disk space of your PC
   B. map of the monitor
   C. space taken up by the monitor on the desk
   D. footprints of the monitor

13. NOS are already built in   13.____
   A. UNIX   B. Mac OS
   C. Windows NT   D. Both A and B

14. _____ is an example of a network monitoring tool.   14.____
   A. Ping   B. VoIP
   C. POP3 server   D. All of the above

15. Tomato is the name of a wireless router   15.____
   A. firmware   B. WRT54GS
   C. both A and B   D. none of the above

16. _____ is a combination of software and hardware.   16.____
   A. Firmware   B. PROM
   C. EPROMs   D. All of the above

17. Object-oriented fonts are also called   17.____
   A. scalable fonts   B. vector fonts
   C. both A and B   D. screen fonts

18. What is the issue if the computer is rebooting itself?   18.____
   A. Faulty power supply   B. Faulty cooling fan
   C. Dirt on the cooling fan   D. All of the above

19. What is the meaning if you receive a message "system running low on   19._____
virtual memory"?
    A. The system is low on RAM   B. The hard disc is full
    C. Both A and B   D. None of the above

20. Your computer freezes on startup. What is the issue?   20._____
    A. Defective hardware   B. Faulty software
    C. Bugged OS   D. All of the above

21. The computer software maintenance checklist consists of   21._____
    A. update virus or install antivirus   B. delete temporary internet file
    C. clear internet cache   D. all of the above

22. A CRC error is caused by   22._____
    A. a scratched DVD on disk   B. dirt on CD/DVD
    C. partially burned CDs   D. all of the above

23. An error message "an invalid Windows File" means   23._____
    A. incomplete download   B. system crash
    C. software bug   D. all of the above

24. What would you do if it is taking longer than usual to copy files in Windows?   24._____
    A. Install an external file such as TeraCopy
    B. Resume broken files
    C. Increase RAM
    D. Both A and B

25. _____ software will help you protect file and folders.   25._____
    A. HideFolder   B. Truecrypt
    C. TeraCopy   D. None of the above

———————

KEY (CORRECT ANSWERS)

1.	D		11.	C
2.	C		12.	C
3.	C		13.	D
4.	A		14.	D
5.	A		15.	A
6.	A		16.	A
7.	A		17.	C
8.	D		18.	D
9.	D		19.	A
10.	D		20.	D

21.	D
22.	D
23.	D
24.	A
25.	B

EXAMINATION SECTION

TEST 1

DIRECTIONS: Each question or incomplete statement is followed by several suggested answers or completions. Select the one that BEST answers the question or completes the statement. *PRINT THE LETTER OF THE CORRECT ANSWER IN THE SPACE AT THE RIGHT.*

1. The SDLC is defined as a process consisting of _____ phases.　　1.____
   A. two　　　　　B. four　　　　　C. three　　　D. five

2. A framework that describes the set of activities performed at each stage of　　2.____
   a software development project is
   A. SDLC　　　　　　　　　　B. deployment
   C. waterfall model　　　　　D. SDLC model

3. How is noise defined in terms of software development?　　3.____
   A. Writing irrelevant statement to the software development in the SRS
      document
   B. Adding clashing requirements in the SRS document
   C. Writing over-specific requirements
   D. Writing information about employees

4. Basically, a SWOT analysis is said to be a strategic　　4.____
   A. analysis　　　B. measure　　　C. goal　　　　D. alignment

5. In the system design phase of the SDLC, _____ is not part of the system's　　5.____
   design phase.
   A. design of alternative systems
   B. writing a systems design report
   C. suggestions of alternative solutions
   D. selection of best system

6. In the system development life cycle, which of the following studies is conducted　　6.____
   to determine the possible organizational resistance for a new system?
   _____ feasibility.
   A. Organizational　　B. Operational　　C. Economic　　D. Employee

7. The _____ model is BEST suited when organization is very keen and　　7.____
   motivated to identify the risk on early stages.
   A. waterfall　　　B. RAD　　　　C. spiral　　　　D. incremental

8. Scope of problem is defined with a　　8.____
   A. critical path method (CPM) chart
   B. project evaluation and review technique (PERT) chart
   C. data flow diagram (DFD)
   D. context diagram

9. _____ is referred to as a method of database distribution in which different portions of the database reside at different nodes in the network.

    A. Splitting   B. Partitioning   C. Replication   D. Dividing

    9._____

10. As a software associate, your client needs an information system that must communicate with existing systems. For that purpose, you need to adopt a design method and accurate linking with the existing system. Your designed system will be

    A. database   B. system interface
    C. help desks   D, design interface

    10._____

11. In entity relation, when primary keys are linked with a foreign key, it forms a _____ relationship between the tables that connect them.

    A. many-to-many   B. one-to-one
    C. parent-child   D. server-and-client

    11._____

12. In normalization, a relation is in a third normal form when no _____ attribute is determining another non-key attribute.

    A. dependent   B. non-key
    C. key   D. none of the above

    12._____

13. In library management databases, which terminology is used to refer to a specific record in your database?

    A. Relation   B. Instance   C. Table   D. Column

    13._____

14. In database, a rule which describes that foreign key value must match with the primary key value in the other relationship is called

    A. referential integrity constraint   B. key match rule
    C. entity key group rule   D. foreign/primary match rule

    14._____

15. The attribute on the left-hand side of the arrow in a functional dependency is known as

    A. candidate key   B. determinant
    C. foreign key   D. primary key

    15._____

16. A report may be based on a

    A. table   B. query
    C. relations   D. both A and B

    16._____

17. A software program which is used to build reports that summarize data from a database is known as

    A. report writer   B. reporter
    C. report builder   D. report generator

    17._____

18. Which one of the following database objects is created FIRST?

    A. Table   B. Form   C. Report   D. Query

    18._____

19. In data structures, a _____-linked list does not contain a null pointer at the end of the list.
    A. circular   B. doubly   C. null   D. stacked

    19._____

20. Polymorphism is described as the
    A. process of returning data from functions by reference
    B. specialization of classes through inheritance
    C. use of classes to represent objects
    D. packaging of data defining an object as a private member variable of class

    20._____

21. In C++, dynamic binding is useful for the functions that are
    A. overridden   B. defined once
    C. undefined   D. bounded

    21._____

22. In programming language, a function template is required when
    A. implementation details of function are independent of parameter data types
    B. all functions should be function templates
    C. two different functions have different implementation details
    D. two functions have the same type of parameters

    22._____

23. _____ are used to group classes for ease of use, maintainability and reusability.
    A. Use cases   B. States   C. Objects   D. Packages

    23._____

24. The description of structure and organization of data in database is contained in
    A. data dictionary   B. data mine
    C. structured query language   D. data mapping

    24._____

25. What is the output of the following programming code?

```
Int p, q, r;
P=10, q=3, r=2,
If (p+q)<14&&(r<q-3)
Cout <<r;
Else
Cout << p;
```

    A. -2   B. 4   C. 10   D. -4

    25._____

KEY (CORRECT ANSWERS)

1.	D		11.	C
2.	D		12.	B
3.	A		13.	B
4.	A		14.	A
5.	C		15.	B
6.	B		16.	D
7.	C		17.	B
8.	D		18.	A
9.	C		19.	A
10.	B		20.	B

21.	A
22.	D
23.	C
24.	A
25.	C

TEST 2

DIRECTIONS: Each question or incomplete statement is followed by several suggested answers or completions. Select the one that BEST answers the question or completes the statement. *PRINT THE LETTER OF THE CORRECT ANSWER IN THE SPACE AT THE RIGHT.*

1. Which of the following is the BEST fact-finding technique that is most helpful in collecting quantitative data?
   A. Interviews
   B. Record reviews and comparisons
   C. Questionnaires
   D. Workshops

   1.____

2. _____ data is a type of data collected from open-ended questions.
   A. Quantitative
   B. Qualitative
   C. Experimental
   D. Non-official

   2.____

3. Usually a feasibility study is carried out
   A. after completion of final requirement specification
   B. before the start of the project
   C. before the completion of final requirements specifications
   D. at any time

   3.____

4. In the analysis phase, which diagram is used to present declaration of the goals and objectives of the project.
   A. Data flow diagram
   B. Entity relationship diagram
   C. Flowchart
   D. Documentation

   4.____

5. In SDLC, _____ is used to ensure that no alternative is ignored during data analysis.
   A. data flow diagram
   B. organizational chart
   C. Gantt chart
   D. decision table

   5.____

6. Which of the following software is used to measure hardware and software alternatives?
   A. Automated design tools
   B. DFD
   C. Report generators
   D. Project management

   6.____

7. _____ is responsible to write Software Requirement Specifications Document (SRS).
   A. Project manager
   B. System analyst
   C. Programmer
   D. User

   7.____

8. An entity which relates to itself in an ERD model is referred to as _____ relationship.
   A. recursive
   B. one-to-many
   C. many-to-many
   D. one-to-one

   8.____

9. The goal of normalization is
   A. to increase the number of relations
   B. to increase redundancy
   C. independence of any other relation
   D. to get stable data structure

9.____

10. CMM stands for
   A. Capability Maturity Model   B. Configuration Maturity Model
   C. Capacity Building Manager   D. Company Management Method

10.____

11. Data _____ is terminology used for data accuracy and completeness in any database.
   A. constraint   B. redundancy   C. model   D. integrity

11.____

12. A candidate key is defined as
   A. a primary key
   B. the primary key selected to be the key of a relation
   C. an attribute or group of attributes that can be a primary key
   D. both A and B

12.____

13. The ability of a class to derive the properties from previously defined class is
   A. encapsulation   B. polymorphism
   C. information hiding   D. inheritance

13.____

14. A queue data structure stores and retrieves items in a _____ manner.
   A. last in, first out   B. first in, last out
   C. first in, first out   D. last in, last out

14.____

15. The process of writing a program from an algorithm is called
   A. coding   B. decoding   C. encoding   D. encrypting

15.____

16. The CORRECT sequence for creating and executing C++ program is:
   A. Compiling-Editing-Saving-Executing-Linking
   B. Editing-Executing-Compiling-Linking
   C. Editing-Saving-Compiling-Linking-Executing
   D. Linking-Executing-Saving-Compiling

16.____

17. As an instructor, you have given your class a programming problem. Every student comes up with a different instruction code for the same problem. Suppose one student has a code of 50 lines, while another has a code of 100 instructions for the same problem.
Which of the following statements is TRUE?
   A. The greater execution time is required for more instructions than that of less instructions.
   B. Execution time of all programs are the same.
   C. The number of instruction codes does not affect the solution.
   D. Compilation time is greater with more numbers of instruction.

17.____

18. In programming languages, a counter can be defined as   18.____
    A. the final value of a loop
    B. a variable that counts loop iterations
    C. the initial value of a loop
    D. the stop value of loop

19. Which reserve word is used in programming languages to move the control   19.____
back to the start of the loop body?
    A. Break   B. Go to   C. Continue   D. Switch

20. The FIRST line in switch block contains the   20.____
    A. value of first criterion
    B. statement to be executed if the first criteria is true
    C. expression to be evaluated
    D. statement to be executed if none of the criteria is true

21. What is the output of the following code?   21.____

```
int main ()
{
    int a = 19;
    {
        cout << "value of a: "<<a<<endl;
        a = a + 1;
    }while(a<20);
    return 0;
}
```

    A. 19   B. 20   C. 11   D. 100

22. A computer dedicated to screening access to a network from outside the   22.____
network is known as
    A. hot site   B. cold site   C. firewall   D. vaccine

23. In anticipation of physical destruction, every organization should have a   23.____
    A. biometric scheme   B. disaster recovery plan
    C. DES   D. set of active plan

24. Debug is a term denoting   24.____
    A. error correction process
    B. writing of instructions in developing a new program
    C. fault detection in equipment
    D. determine useful life

25. A feature of word processing software to link the name and addresses with   25.____
a standard document is called
    A. mail merge   B. database management
    C. references   D. review/comment

KEY (CORRECT ANSWERS)

1.	C	11.	D
2.	B	12.	C
3.	A	13.	D
4.	C	14.	C
5.	D	15.	A
6.	A	16.	C
7.	A	17.	A
8.	A	18.	B
9.	D	19.	C
10.	A	20.	B

21.	A
22.	C
23.	B
24.	A
25.	A

TEST 3

DIRECTIONS: Each question or incomplete statement is followed by several suggested answers or completions. Select the one that BEST answers the question or completes the statement. *PRINT THE LETTER OF THE CORRECT ANSWER IN THE SPACE AT THE RIGHT.*

1. The parallelogram symbol in a flow chart indicates a
   A. process   B. progress   C. condition   D. input/output   1.____

2. A feasibility study in SDLC performs   2.____
   A. cost/benefit analysis
   B. designing technique analysis
   C. debugging selection
   D. programming language selection

3. Who is responsible for performing the feasibility study?   3.____
   A. Organizational managers
   B. Both organizational manager and system analyst
   C. Users of the proposed system
   D. Both perspective user and systems designers

4. A study of employees' working habits, phobias and obsessions during   4.____
   implementation of a new system is called _____ analysis.
   A. personality   B. cultural feasibility
   C. economic feasibility   D. technological feasibility

5. As a software associate, a(n) _____ model is based on a regression testing   5.____
   technique.
   A. waterfall   B. RAD   C. V   D. iterative

6. The adaptable model which describes features of the proposed system and   6.____
   is implemented before the installation of the actual system is known as
   A. JAD   B. template   C. RAD   D. prototype

7. Milestones in system development life cycle represent   7.____
   A. cost of project   B. status of project
   C. user expectation   D. final product of project

8. Scheduling deadlines and milestones can be shown on a   8.____
   A. system survey   B. decision table
   C. prototype   D. Gantt chart

9. Suppose your current organization wants to expand its business into different cities. For that purpose, it needs to distribute business applications across multiple locations. For example, computer systems, storing the data center for Web server, database and telecommunication functions. This is an example of

    A. applications architecture planning
    B. technology architecture planning
    C. enterprise resource planning (ERP)
    D. strategic planning

    9.____

10. All of the following are components of a physical database EXCEPT

    A. file organization   B. data volume
    C. data distribution   D. normalize the relations

    10.____

11. Suppose working as a computer associate your organization has assigned you a task to develop a database for an academic institution. Which one is the MOST appropriate association in the database for a class that might have multiple prerequisites?

    A. Generalization association   B. N-ary association
    C. Aggregation association   D. Reflexive association

    11.____

12. While working on an academic institute database, according to you, which one is the MOST suitable special association to model a course that has an instructor, teaching assistants, a classroom, meeting time slot and class schedule?

    A. Generalization association   B. N-ary association
    C. Aggregation association   D. Reflexive association

    12.____

13. Which one of the following is the MOST suitable association that shows that multiple textbooks for a course are required to make a reading list?

    A. Aggregation association   B. Generalization association
    C. N-ary association   D. Reflexive association

    13.____

14. In parameters, passing by value

    A. actual parameters and formal parameters must be similar types
    B. actual parameters and formal parameters can be different types
    C. parameters passing by value can be used both for input and output purpose
    D. both A and B

    14.____

15. In data structures, which of the following can be used to facilitate adding nodes to the end of the linear linked list?

    A. Head pointer   B. Zero head node
    C. Tail pointer   D. Precede pointer

    15.____

16. A full binary tree with n leaves consist of _____ nodes.

    A. n   B. 2^{n-1} C. n-1   D. log n

    16.____

17.　Linear model and prototyping model are combined to form a _____ model.　　　　17.____
　　　A. waterfall　　　　　　　　　　　B. incremental
　　　C. build & fix　　　　　　　　　　D. spiral

18.　An example of query is　　　　　　　　　　　　　　　　　　　　　　　　　　18.____
　　　A. selection of all records that match a set of criteria
　　　B. importing spreadsheet file into the database
　　　C. search for specific record
　　　D. both A and C are correct

19.　The database development process involves mapping of conceptual data　　　19.____
　　　model into a(n) _____ model.
　　　A. object-oriented　　　　　　　　B. network data
　　　C. implementation　　　　　　　　D. hierarchical data

20.　In database, one field or combination of fields for which more than one　　　20.____
　　　record may have the same combination of values is called the
　　　A. secondary key　　　　　　　　　B. index
　　　C. composite key　　　　　　　　　D. linked key

21.　Customers, cars and parts are examples of　　　　　　　　　　　　　　　　　21.____
　　　A. entities　　　　B. attributes　　　C. cardinals　　　D. relationships

22.　A ping program used to send a multiple packet to a server to check its　　　22.____
　　　ability to handle a quantity of traffic maliciously is called
　　　A. pagejacking　　　　　　　　　　B. jam sync
　　　C. ping storm　　　　　　　　　　　D. ping strangeness

23.　Which one of the following is the key factor to develop a new system to　　　23.____
　　　manage a disaster?
　　　A. Equipment replacement　　　　　B. Unfavorable weather
　　　C. Lack of insurance coverage　　　D. Loss of processing ability

24.　As a computer associate, you ask 100 client organization employees to　　　24.____
　　　fill out a survey that includes questions about educational background, their job
　　　type, salary and amount spent on purchases of a widget annually. After you
　　　enter the data in a spreadsheet program, you decide to look for a relationship
　　　between income and the amount spent on widgets. The BEST way to display
　　　the data for this kind of assumption is a _____ chart.
　　　A. bullet　　　　　B. line　　　　　C. pic　　　　　D. scatter

25.　Suppose it is your very first day of your job. When you turn on your　　　25.____
　　　computer, the system unit is visibly on but the monitor is dark. What is the
　　　exact issue?
　　　A. The monitor model is too old to work
　　　B. The operating system is not working
　　　C. The monitor is not connected to the PC
　　　D. Call the help desk officer

KEY (CORRECT ANSWERS)

1.	D		11.	D
2.	A		12.	B
3.	A		13.	C
4.	B		14.	A
5.	D		15.	C
6.	D		16.	B
7.	B		17.	B
8.	D		18.	D
9.	B		19.	C
10.	D		20.	A

21.	A
22.	C
23.	D
24.	D
25.	C

TEST 4

DIRECTIONS: Each question or incomplete statement is followed by several suggested answers or completions. Select the one that BEST answers the question or completes the statement. *PRINT THE LETTER OF THE CORRECT ANSWER IN THE SPACE AT THE RIGHT.*

1. A collection of logically related data elements that can be used for multiple processing needs is called
   A. files   B. a register   C. a database   D. organization

1.____

2. For the purpose of data gathering, your organization and client have secretly engaged you in the client group that is being studied. You are considered a(n)
   A. observer-as-participant   B. observer
   C. complete participant   D. part-time employee

2.____

3. For data gathering, interviews in which the topics are pre-decided but the sequence and phrasing can be adapted during the interview is called a(n)
   A. informal conversational interview
   B. closed quantitative interview
   C. standardized open-ended interview
   D. interview-guided approach

3.____

4. In SDLC, which of the following analysis methods is adopted to start with the "intricate image" and then breaks it down into smaller sections?
   A. Financial   B. Bottom up   C. Reverse
   D. Top-down   E. Executive

4.____

5. As a software associate, which one of the following is the biggest reason for the failure of system development projects?
   A. Lack of JAD sessions
   B. Purchasing COTS
   C. Imprecise or missing business requirements
   D. Hurdles from employees

5.____

6. The _____ model is the BEST suited model to create client/server applications.
   A. waterfall   B. spiral   C. incremental   D. concurrent

6.____

7. Which hardware component is essential for function of a database management system?
   A. Larger capacity, high speed disk
   B. Mouse
   C. High resolution monitors
   D. Printer

7.____

8. _____ refers to a method of database distribution in which one database contains data that are included in another database.
   A. Splitting   B. Partitioning
   C. Replication   D. Dividing

8.____

9. In the database design process, which one of the following is referred to modality?
    A. Optional   B. Mandatory
    C. Unidirectional   D. Both A and B

9.____

10. According to the research conducted by an international professional organization, out of 100 most occupied jobs that they researched, the top job classification was a
    A. database administrator   B. cryptographer
    C. programmer   D. computer engineer

10.____

11. In the database, different attributes in two different tables having the same name are referred to as
    A. a synonym   B. a homonym
    C. an acronym   D. mutually exclusive

11.____

12. Consider two tables: Class and Student are related by a "one-to-many" relationship. In which table should the corresponding foreign key be placed?
    A. Only Class table requires foreign key.
    B. Only Student table requires foreign key.
    C. Both tables require foreign key.
    D. Composite entity must be added so foreign keys will be required in both Class and Student tables.

12.____

13.

Using the above E-R diagram, which one of the following statements is TRUE?
    A. Both tables should have the same number of (primary) key attributes.
    B. Table A should have a larger number of key attributes.
    C. Table B should have a larger number of key attributes.
    D. The diagram does not propose which table might have more attributes in its primary key.

13.____

14. Which form of functional dependency is the set of attributes that is neither a subset or any of the keys nor the candidate key?
    A. Full functional dependency   B. Partial dependency
    C. Primary functional dependency   D. Transitive dependency

14.____

15. The true dependencies are formed by the _____ rule.
    A. reflexive   B. referential   C. inferential   D. termination

15.____

16. Which facility helps DBMS to synchronize its files and journals while occasionally suspending all processing?
    A. Checkpoint facility   B. Backup recovery
    C. Recovery manager   D. Database change log

16.____

17. In data structures, which one of the following operations is used to retrieve and then remove the top of the stack?
    A. Create Stack
    B. Push
    C. Pop
    D. Pull

17.____

18. Class definition
    A. must have a constructor specified
    B. must end with a semicolon
    C. provides the class interface
    D. both B and C

18.____

19. Which operator is used in compound condition to join two conditions?
    A. Relational operator
    B. Logical operator
    C. Relational result
    D. Logical result

19.____

20. The conditional portion of IF statements can contain any
    A. valid expression
    B. expression that can be evaluated to Boolean value
    C. valid variable
    D. valid constant or variable

20.____

21. System analysts suggest that telecommuting will become more popular with managers and client teams when
    A. workers are forced to telecommute
    B. the manager finally gives up the idea of controlling the worker
    C. multimedia teleconferencing system becomes affordable
    D. automobiles become outdated

21.____

22. Error reports are an example of _____ reports.
    A. scheduled
    B. exception
    C. on-demand
    D. external

22.____

23. Word processing, electronic filling, and electronic mails are part of
    A. help desk
    B. electronic industry
    C. office automation
    D. official tasks

23.____

24. In a word processor, the block that appears at the top and bottom of every page which display deals is called the
    A. top and bottom margin
    B. headline and end note
    C. title and page number
    D. header and footer

24.____

25. In word processing software, _____ are inserted as a cross-reference.
    A. placeholders
    B. bookmarks
    C. objects
    D. word fields

25.____

KEY (CORRECT ANSWERS)

1.	C		11.	C
2.	C		12.	B
3.	D		13.	D
4.	B		14.	D
5.	C		15.	A
6.	D		16.	A
7.	A		17.	C
8.	C		18.	A
9.	D		19.	D
10.	D		20.	A

21.	C
22.	B
23.	C
24.	D
25.	D

EXAMINATION SECTION

TEST 1

DIRECTIONS: Each question or incomplete statement is followed by several suggested answers or completions. Select the one that BEST answers the question or completes the statement. *PRINT THE LETTER OF THE CORRECT ANSWER IN THE SPACE AT THE RIGHT.*

1. Which of the following is the BEST fact-finding technique that is most helpful in collecting quantitative data?
   A. Interviews
   B. Record reviews and comparisons
   C. Questionnaires
   D. Workshops

   1.____

2. _____ data is a type of data collected from open-ended questions.
   A. Quantitative
   B. Qualitative
   C. Experimental
   D. Non-official

   2.____

3. Usually a feasibility study is carried out
   A. after completion of final requirement specification
   B. before the start of the project
   C. before the completion of final requirements specifications
   D. at any time

   3.____

4. In the analysis phase, which diagram is used to present declaration of the goals and objectives of the project.
   A. Data flow diagram
   B. Entity relationship diagram
   C. Flowchart
   D. Documentation

   4.____

5. In SDLC, _____ is used to ensure that no alternative is ignored during data analysis.
   A. data flow diagram
   B. organizational chart
   C. Gantt chart
   D. decision table

   5.____

6. Which of the following software is used to measure hardware and software alternatives?
   A. Automated design tools
   B. DFD
   C. Report generators
   D. Project management

   6.____

7. _____ is responsible to write Software Requirement Specifications Document (SRS).
   A. Project manager
   B. System analyst
   C. Programmer
   D. User

   7.____

8. An entity which relates to itself in an ERD model is referred to as _____ relationship.
   A. recursive
   B. one-to-many
   C. many-to-many
   D. one-to-one

   8.____

9. The goal of normalization is   9._____
    A. to increase the number of relations
    B. to increase redundancy
    C. independence of any other relation
    D. to get stable data structure

10. CMM stands for   10._____
    A. Capability Maturity Model   B. Configuration Maturity Model
    C. Capacity Building Manager   D. Company Management Method

11. Data _____ is terminology used for data accuracy and completeness in any   11._____
    database.
    A. constraint   B. redundancy   C. model   D. integrity

12. A candidate key is defined as   12._____
    A. a primary key
    B. the primary key selected to be the key of a relation
    C. an attribute or group of attributes that can be a primary key
    D. both A and B

13. The ability of a class to derive the properties from previously defined class   13._____
    is
    A. encapsulation   B. polymorphism
    C. information hiding   D. inheritance

14. A queue data structure stores and retrieves items in a _____ manner.   14._____
    A. last in, first out   B. first in, last out
    C. first in, first out   D. last in, last out

15. The process of writing a program from an algorithm is called   15._____
    A. coding   B. decoding   C. encoding   D. encrypting

16. The CORRECT sequence for creating and executing C++ program is: 16._____
    A. Compiling-Editing-Saving-Executing-Linking
    B. Editing-Executing-Compiling-Linking
    C. Editing-Saving-Compiling-Linking-Executing
    D. Linking-Executing-Saving-Compiling

17. As an instructor, you have given your class a programming problem.   17._____
    Every student comes up with a different instruction code for the same problem.
    Suppose one student has a code of 50 lines, while another has a code of 100
    instructions for the same problem.
    Which of the following statements is TRUE?
    A. The greater execution time is required for more instructions than that of
       less instructions.
    B. Execution time of all programs are the same.
    C. The number of instruction codes does not affect the solution.
    D. Compilation time is greater with more numbers of instruction.

18. In programming languages, a counter can be defined as   18.____
    A. the final value of a loop
    B. a variable that counts loop iterations
    C. the initial value of a loop
    D. the stop value of loop

19. Which reserve word is used in programming languages to move the control   19.____
    back to the start of the loop body?
    A. Break   B. Go to   C. Continue   D. Switch

20. The FIRST line in switch block contains the   20.____
    A. value of first criterion
    B. statement to be executed if the first criteria is true
    C. expression to be evaluated
    D. statement to be executed if none of the criteria is true

21. What is the output of the following code?   21.____

```
int main ()
{
    int a = 19;
    {
        cout << "value of a: "<<a<<endl;
        a = a + 1;
    }while(a<20);
    return 0;
}
```

    A. 19   B. 20   C. 11   D. 100

22. A computer dedicated to screening access to a network from outside the   22.____
    network is known as
    A. hot site   B. cold site   C. firewall   D. vaccine

23. In anticipation of physical destruction, every organization should have a   23.____
    A. biometric scheme   B. disaster recovery plan
    C. DES   D. set of active plan

24. Debug is a term denoting   24.____
    A. error correction process
    B. writing of instructions in developing a new program
    C. fault detection in equipment
    D. determine useful life

25. A feature of word processing software to link the name and addresses with   25.____
    a standard document is called
    A. mail merge   B. database management
    C. references   D. review/comment

KEY (CORRECT ANSWERS)

1.	C		11.	D
2.	B		12.	C
3.	A		13.	D
4.	C		14.	C
5.	D		15.	A
6.	A		16.	C
7.	A		17.	A
8.	A		18.	B
9.	D		19.	C
10.	A		20.	B

21.	A
22.	C
23.	B
24.	A
25.	A

————————

TEST 2

DIRECTIONS: Each question or incomplete statement is followed by several suggested answers or completions. Select the one that BEST answers the question or completes the statement. *PRINT THE LETTER OF THE CORRECT ANSWER IN THE SPACE AT THE RIGHT.*

1. The SDLC is defined as a process consisting of _____ phases.
   A. two   B. four   C. three   D. five

   1._____

2. A framework that describes the set of activities performed at each stage of a software development project is
   A. SDLC   B. deployment
   C. waterfall model   D. SDLC model

   2._____

3. How is noise defined in terms of software development?
   A. Writing irrelevant statement to the software development in the SRS document
   B. Adding clashing requirements in the SRS document
   C. Writing over-specific requirements
   D. Writing information about employees

   3._____

4. Basically, a SWOT analysis is said to be a strategic
   A. analysis   B. measure   C. goal   D. alignment

   4._____

5. In the system design phase of the SDLC, _____ is not part of the system's design phase.
   A. design of alternative systems
   B. writing a systems design report
   C. suggestions of alternative solutions
   D. selection of best system

   5._____

6. In the system development life cycle, which of the following studies is conducted to determine the possible organizational resistance for a new system? _____ feasibility.
   A. Organizational   B. Operational   C. Economic   D. Employee

   6._____

7. The _____ model is BEST suited when organization is very keen and motivated to identify the risk on early stages.
   A. waterfall   B. RAD   C. spiral   D. incremental

   7._____

8. Scope of problem is defined with a
   A. critical path method (CPM) chart
   B. project evaluation and review technique (PERT) chart
   C. data flow diagram (DFD)
   D. context diagram

   8._____

9. _____ is referred to as a method of database distribution in which different portions of the database reside at different nodes in the network.

    A. Splitting   B. Partitioning   C. Replication   D. Dividing

9.____

10. As a computer specialist (software), your client needs an information system that must communicate with existing systems. For that purpose, you need to adopt a design method and accurate linking with the existing system. Your designed system will be

    A. database   B. system interface
    C. help desks   D, design interface

10.____

11. In entity relation, when primary keys are linked with a foreign key, it forms a _____ relationship between the tables that connect them.

    A. many-to-many   B. one-to-one
    C. parent-child   D. server-and-client

11.____

12. In normalization, a relation is in a third normal form when no _____ attribute is determining another non-key attribute.

    A. dependent   B. non-key
    C. key   D. none of the above

12.____

13. In library management databases, which terminology is used to refer to a specific record in your database?

    A. Relation   B. Instance   C. Table   D. Column

13.____

14. In database, a rule which describes that foreign key value must match with the primary key value in the other relationship is called

    A. referential integrity constraint   B. key match rule
    C. entity key group rule   D. foreign/primary match rule

14.____

15. The attribute on the left-hand side of the arrow in a functional dependency is known as

    A. candidate key   B. determinant
    C. foreign key   D. primary key

15.____

16. A report may be based on a

    A. table   B. query
    C. relations   D. both A and B

16.____

17. A software program which is used to build reports that summarize data from a database is known as

    A. report writer   B. reporter
    C. report builder   D. report generator

17.____

18. Which one of the following database objects is created FIRST?

    A. Table   B. Form   C. Report   D. Query

18.____

19. In data structures, a _____-linked list does not contain a null pointer at the end of the list.
    A. circular   B. doubly   C. null   D. stacked

19._____

20. Polymorphism is described as the
    A. process of returning data from functions by reference
    B. specialization of classes through inheritance
    C. use of classes to represent objects
    D. packaging of data defining an object as a private member variable of class

20._____

21. In C++, dynamic binding is useful for the functions that are
    A. overridden   B. defined once
    C. undefined   D. bounded

21._____

22. In programming language, a function template is required when
    A. implementation details of function are independent of parameter data types
    B. all functions should be function templates
    C. two different functions have different implementation details
    D. two functions have the same type of parameters

22._____

23. _____ are used to group classes for ease of use, maintainability and reusability.
    A. Use cases   B. States   C. Objects   D. Packages

23._____

24. The description of structure and organization of data in database is contained in
    A. data dictionary   B. data mine
    C. structured query language   D. data mapping

24._____

25. What is the output of the following programming code?
```
Int p, q, r;
P=10, q=3, r=2,
If (p+q)<14&&(r<q-3)
Cout ≪r;
Else
Cout ≪ p;
```

    A. -2   B. 4   C. 10   D. -4

25._____

KEY (CORRECT ANSWERS)

1.	D		11.	C
2.	D		12.	B
3.	A		13.	B
4.	A		14.	A
5.	C		15.	B
6.	B		16.	D
7.	C		17.	B
8.	D		18.	A
9.	C		19.	A
10.	B		20.	B

21.	A
22.	D
23.	C
24.	A
25.	C

TEST 3

DIRECTIONS: Each question or incomplete statement is followed by several suggested answers or completions. Select the one that BEST answers the question or completes the statement. *PRINT THE LETTER OF THE CORRECT ANSWER IN THE SPACE AT THE RIGHT.*

1. The parallelogram symbol in a flow chart indicates a   1.____
   A. process   B. progress   C. condition   D. input/output

2. A feasibility study in SDLC performs   2.____
   A. cost/benefit analysis
   B. designing technique analysis
   C. debugging selection
   D. programming language selection

3. Who is responsible for performing the feasibility study?   3.____
   A. Organizational managers
   B. Both organizational manager and system analyst
   C. Users of the proposed system
   D. Both perspective user and systems designers

4. A study of employees' working habits, phobias and obsessions during   4.____
   implementation of a new system is called _____ analysis.
   A. personality   B. cultural feasibility
   C. economic feasibility   D. technological feasibility

5. As a computer specialist (software), a(n) _____ model is based on a regression   5.____
   testing technique.
   A. waterfall   B. RAD   C. V   D. iterative

6. The adaptable model which describes features of the proposed system and   6.____
   is implemented before the installation of the actual system is known as
   A. JAD   B. template   C. RAD   D. prototype

7. Milestones in system development life cycle represent   7.____
   A. cost of project   B. status of project
   C. user expectation   D. final product of project

8. Scheduling deadlines and milestones can be shown on a   8.____
   A. system survey   B. decision table
   C. prototype   D. Gantt chart

9. Suppose your current organization wants to expand its business into different cities. For that purpose, it needs to distribute business applications across multiple locations. For example, computer systems, storing the data center for Web server, database and telecommunication functions. This is an example of
   A. applications architecture planning
   B. technology architecture planning
   C. enterprise resource planning (ERP)
   D. strategic planning

9.____

10. All of the following are components of a physical database EXCEPT
    A. file organization   B. data volume
    C. data distribution   D. normalize the relations

10.____

11. Suppose working as a computer specialist (software) your organization has assigned you a task to develop a database for an academic institution. Which one is the MOST appropriate association in the database for a class that might have multiple prerequisites?
    A. Generalization association   B. N-ary association
    C. Aggregation association   D. Reflexive association

11.____

12. While working on an academic institute database, according to you, which one is the MOST suitable special association to model a course that has an instructor, teaching assistants, a classroom, meeting time slot and class schedule?
    A. Generalization association   B. N-ary association
    C. Aggregation association   D. Reflexive association

12.____

13. Which one of the following is the MOST suitable association that shows that multiple textbooks for a course are required to make a reading list?
    A. Aggregation association   B. Generalization association
    C. N-ary association   D. Reflexive association

13.____

14. In parameters, passing by value
    A. actual parameters and formal parameters must be similar types
    B. actual parameters and formal parameters can be different types
    C. parameters passing by value can be used both for input and output purpose
    D. both A and B

14.____

15. In data structures, which of the following can be used to facilitate adding nodes to the end of the linear linked list?
    A. Head pointer   B. Zero head node
    C. Tail pointer   D. Precede pointer

15.____

16. A full binary tree with n leaves consist of _____ nodes.
    A. n   B. 2^{n-1} C. n-1   D. log n

16.____

17. Linear model and prototyping model are combined to form a _____ model.   17.____
    A. waterfall   B. incremental
    C. build & fix   D. spiral

18. An example of query is   18.____
    A. selection of all records that match a set of criteria
    B. importing spreadsheet file into the database
    C. search for specific record
    D. both A and C are correct

19. The database development process involves mapping of conceptual data   19.____
    model into a(n) _____ model.
    A. object-oriented   B. network data
    C. implementation   D. hierarchical data

20. In database, one field or combination of fields for which more than one   20.____
    record may have the same combination of values is called the
    A. secondary key   B. index
    C. composite key   D. linked key

21. Customers, cars and parts are examples of   21.____
    A. entities   B. attributes   C. cardinals   D. relationships

22. A ping program used to send a multiple packet to a server to check its   22.____
    ability to handle a quantity of traffic maliciously is called
    A. pagejacking   B. jam sync
    C. ping storm   D. ping strangeness

23. Which one of the following is the key factor to develop a new system to   23.____
    manage a disaster?
    A. Equipment replacement   B. Unfavorable weather
    C. Lack of insurance coverage   D. Loss of processing ability

24. As a computer specialist (software), you ask 100 client organization employees to   24.____
    fill out a survey that includes questions about educational background, their job
    type, salary and amount spent on purchases of a widget annually. After you
    enter the data in a spreadsheet program, you decide to look for a relationship
    between income and the amount spent on widgets. The BEST way to display
    the data for this kind of assumption is a _____ chart.
    A. bullet   B. line   C. pic   D. scatter

25. Suppose it is your very first day of your job. When you turn on your   25.____
    computer, the system unit is visibly on but the monitor is dark. What is the
    exact issue?
    A. The monitor model is too old to work
    B. The operating system is not working
    C. The monitor is not connected to the PC
    D. Call the help desk officer

KEY (CORRECT ANSWERS)

1.	D		11.	D
2.	A		12.	B
3.	A		13.	C
4.	B		14.	A
5.	D		15.	C
6.	D		16.	B
7.	B		17.	B
8.	D		18.	D
9.	B		19.	C
10.	D		20.	A

21.	A
22.	C
23.	D
24.	D
25.	C

TEST 4

DIRECTIONS: Each question or incomplete statement is followed by several suggested answers or completions. Select the one that BEST answers the question or completes the statement. *PRINT THE LETTER OF THE CORRECT ANSWER IN THE SPACE AT THE RIGHT.*

1. A collection of logically related data elements that can be used for multiple processing needs is called
   A. files   B. a register   C. a database   D. organization

   1.____

2. For the purpose of data gathering, your organization and client have secretly engaged you in the client group that is being studied. You are considered a(n)
   A. observer-as-participant   B. observer
   C. complete participant   D. part-time employee

   2.____

3. For data gathering, interviews in which the topics are pre-decided but the sequence and phrasing can be adapted during the interview is called a(n)
   A. informal conversational interview
   B. closed quantitative interview
   C. standardized open-ended interview
   D. interview-guided approach

   3.____

4. In SDLC, which of the following analysis methods is adopted to start with the "intricate image" and then breaks it down into smaller sections?
   A. Financial   B. Bottom up   C. Reverse
   D. Top-down   E. Executive

   4.____

5. As a computer specialist (software), which one of the following is the biggest reason for the failure of system development projects?
   A. Lack of JAD sessions
   B. Purchasing COTS
   C. Imprecise or missing business requirements
   D. Hurdles from employees

   5.____

6. The _____ model is the BEST suited model to create client/server applications.
   A. waterfall   B. spiral   C. incremental   D. concurrent

   6.____

7. Which hardware component is essential for function of a database management system?
   A. Larger capacity, high speed disk
   B. Mouse
   C. High resolution monitors
   D. Printer

   7.____

8. _____ refers to a method of database distribution in which one database contains data that are included in another database.
   A. Splitting   B. Partitioning
   C. Replication   D. Dividing

   8.____

9. In the database design process, which one of the following is referred to modality?   9.____
    A. Optional   B. Mandatory
    C. Unidirectional   D. Both A and B

10. According to the research conducted by an international professional organization, out of 100 most occupied jobs that they researched, the top job classification was a   10.____
    A. database administrator   B. cryptographer
    C. programmer   D. computer engineer

11. In the database, different attributes in two different tables having the same name are referred to as   11.____
    A. a synonym   B. a homonym
    C. an acronym   D. mutually exclusive

12. Consider two tables: Class and Student are related by a "one-to-many" relationship. In which table should the corresponding foreign key be placed?   12.____
    A. Only Class table requires foreign key.
    B. Only Student table requires foreign key.
    C. Both tables require foreign key.
    D. Composite entity must be added so foreign keys will be required in both Class and Student tables.

13.   13.____

Using the above E-R diagram, which one of the following statements is TRUE?
    A. Both tables should have the same number of (primary) key attributes.
    B. Table A should have a larger number of key attributes.
    C. Table B should have a larger number of key attributes.
    D. The diagram does not propose which table might have more attributes in its primary key.

14. Which form of functional dependency is the set of attributes that is neither a subset or any of the keys nor the candidate key?   14.____
    A. Full functional dependency   B. Partial dependency
    C. Primary functional dependency D. Transitive dependency

15. The true dependencies are formed by the _____ rule.   15.____
    A. reflexive   B. referential   C. inferential   D. termination

16. Which facility helps DBMS to synchronize its files and journals while occasionally suspending all processing?   16.____
    A. Checkpoint facility   B. Backup recovery
    C. Recovery manager   D. Database change log

17. In data structures, which one of the following operations is used to retrieve and then remove the top of the stack?
    A. Create Stack
    B. Push
    C. Pop
    D. Pull

17.____

18. Class definition
    A. must have a constructor specified
    B. must end with a semicolon
    C. provides the class interface
    D. both B and C

18.____

19. Which operator is used in compound condition to join two conditions?
    A. Relational operator
    B. Logical operator
    C. Relational result
    D. Logical result

19.____

20. The conditional portion of IF statements can contain any
    A. valid expression
    B. expression that can be evaluated to Boolean value
    C. valid variable
    D. valid constant or variable

20.____

21. System analysts suggest that telecommuting will become more popular with managers and client teams when
    A. workers are forced to telecommute
    B. the manager finally gives up the idea of controlling the worker
    C. multimedia teleconferencing system becomes affordable
    D. automobiles become outdated

21.____

22. Error reports are an example of _____ reports.
    A. scheduled
    B. exception
    C. on-demand
    D. external

22.____

23. Word processing, electronic filling, and electronic mails are part of
    A. help desk
    B. electronic industry
    C. office automation
    D. official tasks

23.____

24. In a word processor, the block that appears at the top and bottom of every page which display deals is called the
    A. top and bottom margin
    B. headline and end note
    C. title and page number
    D. header and footer

24.____

25. In word processing software, _____ are inserted as a cross-reference.
    A. placeholders
    B. bookmarks
    C. objects
    D. word fields

25.____

KEY (CORRECT ANSWERS)

1.	C		11.	C
2.	C		12.	B
3.	D		13.	D
4.	B		14.	D
5.	C		15.	A
6.	D		16.	A
7.	A		17.	C
8.	C		18.	A
9.	D		19.	D
10.	D		20.	A

21.	C
22.	B
23.	C
24.	D
25.	D

EXAMINATION SECTION

TEST 1

DIRECTIONS: Each question or incomplete statement is followed by several suggested answers or completions. Select the one that BEST answers the question or completes the statement. *PRINT THE LETTER OF THE CORRECT ANSWER IN THE SPACE AT THE RIGHT.*

1. Cardinality in a relational model refers to numbers of   1.____
   A. tuples   B. attributes   C. tables   D. constraints

2. The "AS" clause in SQL is used for which operation?   2.____
   A. Selection   B. Rename   C. Join   D. Projection

3. Database code is written in   3.____
   A. HLL   B. DML   C. DDL   D. DCL

4. In a hierarchical model, records are organized in   4.____
   A. graph   B. list   C. links   D. tree

5. In the entity integrity, the primary key has the value   5.____
   A. not null   B. null
   C. both null and not null   D. any value

6. The tuple relational calculus P1®P2 stands for   6.____
   A. ¬P1 Ú P2   B. P1 Ú P2   C. P1 Ù P2   D. P1 Ù¬P2

7. The method of key transformation is known as   7.____
   A. direct   B. hash   C. random   D. sequential

8. The file organization with fast access to any arbitrary record of a file is   8.____
   A. ordered file   B. unordered file
   C. hashed file   D. B-tree

9. In E-R diagram attributed is symbolized by   9.____
   A. ellipse   B. dashed ellipse
   C. rectangle   D. triangle

10. The operator used to compare a value to a list of literal values is   10.____
   A. BETWEEN   B. ANY   C. IN   D. ALL

11. B-tree of order m has maximum children of   11.____
   A. m   B. m+1   C. m-1   D. m/2

12. The function that divides one numeric expression by another and returns the remainder is,   12.____
   A. POWER   B. MOD   C. ROUND   D. REMAINDER

13. A reflexive association is drawn by   13.____
    A. a line   B. small closed diamond
    B. small open diamond   D. small triangle at the end of a line

14. The special association that indicates multiple textbooks with a course is   14.____
    _____ association.
    A. aggregation   B. generalization
    C. n-ary   D. reflexive

15. In a reflexive association, one class is   15.____
    A. broken down into special cases
    B. combined with multiple other classes
    C. combined with one other class
    D. linked back to itself

16. The technique of defining common properties or functions in the higher class   16.____
    and then modifying them in the lower classes is called
    A. inheritance   B. polymorphism
    C. reflexive   D. transformance

17. Hiding manager's information from the employees is data hiding at   17.____
    A. conceptual level   B. physical level
    C. external level   D. none of the above

18. Versatile report provides   18.____
    A. columnar totals   B. subtotals
    C. calculations   D. all of the above

19. A locked file is   19.____
    A. accessed by one user
    B. modified by users having passwords
    C. used to hide sensitive information
    D. both B and C

20. The SQL command that modifies the rows of tables is known as   20.____
    A. update   B. insert   C. browse   D. append

21. Which one is NOT an aggregate function?   21.____
    A. AVG   B. SUM   C. UPPER   D. MAX

22. In replacing the relation section with some other relation, the initial step is   22.____
    A. delete section   B. drop section
    C. delete from section   D. replace section with new table

23. Which is NOT a relational database?   23.____
    A. dBase IV   B. 4th Dimension
    C. FoxPro   D. Reflex

24. A grouped report is a type of report   24._____
    A. generated by the Report Wizard
    B. that presents records sorted in ascending or descending order as you specify
    C. that displays data grouped by fields you specify
    D. none of the above

25. The output of (100202,Drake,Biology,30000) is   25._____
    A. row(s) inserted   B. error in ID of insert
    C. error in name of insert   D. error in salary of the insert

———————

KEY (CORRECT ANSWERS)

1.	A		11.	A
2.	B		12.	B
3.	C		13.	B
4.	D		14.	D
5.	A		15.	D
6.	B		16.	B
7.	B		17.	C
8.	C		18.	D
9.	B		19.	A
10.	A		20.	A

21.	C
22.	B
23.	D
24.	C
25.	B

———————

TEST 2

DIRECTIONS: Each question or incomplete statement is followed by several suggested answers or completions. Select the one that BEST answers the question or completes the statement. *PRINT THE LETTER OF THE CORRECT ANSWER IN THE SPACE AT THE RIGHT.*

1. The name of a procedural language is
   A. domain relational calculus
   B. tuple relational calculus
   C. relational algebra
   D. query language

   1.____

2. The statement Select* from employee is
   A. DML
   B. DDL
   C. View
   D. Integrity constraint

   2.____

3. The Delete from 5; r- relation will
   A. remove relation
   B. clear relation entries
   C. delete fields
   D. delete rows

   3.____

4. The embedded SQL in COBOL is
   A. EXEC SQL;
   B. EXEC SQL END-EXEC
   C. EXEC SQL
   D. EXEC SQL END EXEC;

   4.____

5. Protocols that ensure conflict safety from deadlocks are
   A. two-phase locking protocol
   B. time-stamp ordering protocol
   C. graph based protocol
   D. both A and B above

   5.____

6. To reduce the process time of remote backup, we use
   A. flags
   B. breakpoints
   C. redo points
   D. checkpoints

   6.____

7. Sort and Filter group commands are in the _____ ribbon.
   A. Home
   B. Create
   C. Tools
   D. Fields

   7.____

8. The options Relationship and SQL Server are placed in the _____ tab.
   A. External Data
   B. Database Tools
   C. Create
   D. Home

   8.____

9. You cannot drop a table if a Drop Table has a constraint of the _____ key.
   A. local
   B. primary
   C. composite
   D. foreign

   9.____

10. Transaction can persist crashes by using the property of
    A. atomicity
    B. durability
    C. isolation
    D. all of the above

    10.____

11. Integrity constraints are defined in the language
    A. DDL Right
    B. DCL
    C. DML
    D. none of the above

    11.____

12. A group of commands collectively performing a function is   12.____
    A. procedure   B. transaction right!
    C. query   D. function

13. Poor administration of data leads to   13.____
    A. same data entity with single definition
    B. familiarity of existing data
    C. data elements missing
    D. all of the above

14. The intrusion detection system does not perform   14.____
    A. identification of hacking attempt into a system
    B. monitoring transfer of packets over the network
    C. transmitting the message packets to destination
    D. establishing deception systems to trap hackers

15. Hypertext Transfer Protocol (HTTP) defines the   15.____
    A. protocol to copy files between computers
    B. transfer protocol to transfer web pages to a browser
    C. database access protocol for SQL statements
    D. hardware/software protocol that limits access to company data

16. A CASE SQL statement defines   16.____
    A. an IF-THEN-ELSE in SQL   B. a loop in SQL
    C. data definition in SQL   D. all of the above

17. Routines and triggers define   17.____
    A. procedural code   B. a call to operate
    C. automatic run   D. storage in the database

18. To join tables, we take the approach of   18.____
    A. subqueries   B. union join
    C. natural join   D. all of the above

19. Backward recovery defines   19.____
    A. before-images applied to the database
    B. after-images applied to the database
    C. after-images and before-images applied to the database
    D. switching to an existing copy of the database

20. Locking may cause   20.____
    A. erroneous updates   B. deadlock
    C. versioning   D. all of the above

21. After a system failure, you recover a database through   21.____
    A. rollback   B. rollforward
    C. switch to duplicate database   D. reprocess transactions

22. Read-only databases are _____ updated.   22.____
    A. always   B. commonly   C. seldom   D. never

23. In order to secure a database, an administrative policy must consider   23.____
    A. authentication policies
    B. limiting access to only authorized people
    C. ensuring appropriate response rates are in external maintenance
       agreements
    D. all of the above

24. Data management technology does not include   24.____
    A. relational   B. rational
    C. object-oriented   D. dimensional

25. SQL INSERT statement defines   25.____
    A. rows modified according to criteria only
    B. mass of rows which cannot be copied from one table to another only
    C. rows inserted into a table only one at a time
    D. rows inserted into a table one at a time or in groups

KEY (CORRECT ANSWERS)

1.	C		11.	A
2.	A		12.	B
3.	C		13.	C
4.	B		14.	C
5.	B		15.	B
6.	D		16.	A
7.	A		17.	A
8.	B		18.	D
9.	D		19.	A
10.	B		20.	B

21.	C
22.	D
23.	D
24.	B
25.	D

TEST 3

1. Which one is NOT a component of a database?   1._____
   A. User data   B. Metadata   C. Reports   D. Indexes

2. The commercial website Amazon.com is an example of _____ database   2._____
   application.
   A. single-user   B. multi-user
   C. e-commerce   D. data mining

3. Which of the following products was the FIRST to implement true relational   3._____
   algebra in a PC DBMS?
   A. IDMS   B. Oracle   C. dBase-II   D. R:base

4. SQL stands for _____ Language.   4._____
   A. Structured Query   B. Sequential Query
   C. Structured Question   D. Sequential Question

5. DBMS function is not used to   5._____
   A. create and process forms   B. create databases
   C. process data   D. administer databases

6. Which function assists people to keep track of their things?   6._____
   A. Database   B. Table   C. Instance   D. Relationship

7. In an ODBC environment, a mediator between application and the DBMS   7._____
   drivers is
   A. data source   B. driver
   C. driver manager   D. OLE DB

8. An Enterprise Resource Planning application is a(n) _____ database application.   8._____
   A. single-user   B. multi-user
   C. e-commerce   D. data mining

9. The use of ID-dependent entities defines   9._____
   A. association relationships only
   B. multi-valued attributes only
   C. archetype/instance relationships only
   D. all of the above use ID dependent entities

10. The entity identifier in a table is   10._____
    A. foreign key   B. main attribute
    C. primary key   D. identity key

11. Which is FALSE for surrogate keys?   11._____
    A. They are short   B. They are fixed
    C. They have meaning to the user   D. They are numeric

12. Minimum cardinalities for every relationship is   12._____
    A. two   B. three   C. four   D. six

13. VPD provides authorization, and the mechanism is called   13._____
    A. row-level authorization   B. column-level authorization
    C. row-type authentication   D. authorization security

14. ON UPDATE CASCADE ensures   14._____
    A. normalization   B. data integrity
    C. materialized views   D. all of the above

15. SQL for an index is   15._____
    A. CREATE INDEX ID;   B. CHANGE INDEX ID;
    C. ADD INDEX ID;   D. REMOVE INDEX ID;

16. The sub-query bracket of an SQL SELECT statement is   16._____
    A. Braces – {...}   B. CAPITAL LETTERS
    C. parenthesis – (...)   D. brackets – [...]

17. Five built-in functions provided by SQL are   17._____
    A. COUNT, SUM, AVG, MAX, MIN   B. SUM, AVG, MIN, MAX, MULT
    C. SUM, AVG, MULT, DIV, MIN   D. SUM, AVG, MIN, MAX, NAME

18. The Microsoft Access wildcards are   18._____
    A. asterisk (*); percent sign (%)   B. percent sign (%); underscore (_)
    C. underscore (_); question mark (?) D. question mark (?); asterisk (*)

19. The function used to sort rows in SQL is   19._____
    A. SORT BY   B. ALIGN BY
    C. ORDER BY   D. GROUP BY

20. EXISTS keyword defines   20._____
    A. only one row in the sub-query meets the condition
    B. all rows in the sub-query fail the condition
    C. both A and B
    D. none of the above

21. In SQL Server 2000, the parameters used in stored procedures are indicated   21._____
    with
    A. #   B. %   C. &   D. @

22. Trigger supported by SQL Server is   22._____
    A. INSTEAD OF only   B. AFTER only
    C. BEFORE only   D. INSTEAD OF and AFTER only

23. Which function in SQL Server 2000 tracks copy of changes since the last   23.____
backup in the database?
     A. Complete backup   B. Transaction log
     C. Differential backup   D. None of the above

24. The transaction log defines the ____ of a record.   24.____
     A. before-image   B. after-image
     C. before and after-image   D. essential data

25. Database is recovered by   25.____
     A. rollback   B. rollforward
     C. switch to duplicate database   D. reprocess transactions

KEY (CORRECT ANSWERS)

1.	C		11.	C
2.	C		12.	D
3.	D		13.	A
4.	A		14.	B
5.	A		15.	A
6.	A		16.	C
7.	C		17.	A
8.	B		18.	D
9.	D		19.	C
10.	C		20.	A

21.	D
22.	D
23.	C
24.	D
25.	C

TEST 4

DIRECTIONS: Each question or incomplete statement is followed by several suggested answers or completions. Select the one that BEST answers the question or completes the statement. *PRINT THE LETTER OF THE CORRECT ANSWER IN THE SPACE AT THE RIGHT.*

1. A relational database includes a collection of   1.____
    A. tables   B. fields   C. records   D. keys

2. A domain is said to be atomic if elements are   2.____
    A. different   B. indivisible   C. constant   D. divisible

3. The statement Course(course_id,sec_id,semester) course_id,sec_id and   3.____
    semester are defined as
    A. relations, attribute   B. attributes, relation
    C. tuple, relation   D. tuple, attributes

4. Each entity has a descriptive property called   4.____
    A. entity   B. attribute   C. relation   D. model

5. The structure of the relation, deleting relation, and relating schemas is   5.____
    defined in
    A. DML (Data Manipulation Language)
    B. DDL (Data Definition Language)
    C. Query
    D. Relational Schema

6. To query information and to insert tuples, delete tuples, and modify tuples we   6.____
    use
    A. DML (Data Manipulation Language)
    B. DDL (Data Definition Language)
    C. Query
    D. Relational Schema

7. Which function is used to remove a relation from an SQL database?   7.____
    A. Delete   B. Purge   C. Remove   D. Drop Table

8. Insert into instructor values (10211,'Smith','Biology',66000); defines   8.____
    A. Query   B. DML   C. Relational   D. DDL

9. To append two strings, we use operator   9.____
    A. &   B. %   C. □   D. _

10. In the DBMS environment, Date format is   10.____
    A. mm/dd/yy   B. yyyy/mm/dd   C. dd/mm/yy   D. yy/dd/mm

11. SQL store movie and image files by data type: 11.____
    A. clob   B. blob   C. binary   D. image

12. Hashing search defines _____ time. 12.____
    A. O(1)   B. O(n2)   C. O(log n)   D. O(n log n)

13. Key value pairs defines 13.____
    A. hash tables   B. heaps   C. both A and B   D. skip list

14. Breadth First Search is 14.____
    A. binary trees   B. stacks
    C. graphs   D. both A and C above

15. We identify deleted records by _____ bitmap. 15.____
    A. existence   B. current   C. final   D. deleted

16. The oldest database model is 16.____
    A. relational   B. deductive   C. physical   D. network

17. Snapshot isolation defines 17.____
    A. concurrency-control   B. concurrency-allowance
    C. redirection   D. repetition-allowance

18. A condition in SQL is 18.____
    A. join in SQL   B. join condition
    C. both of the above   D. none of the above

19. The operation allowed in a join view is 19.____
    A. UPDATE   B. INSERT
    C. DELETE   D. all of the above

20. Concurrency control on B+ trees is used to 20.____
    A. remove unwanted data   B. easily add the index elements
    C. maintain accuracy of index   D. all of the above

21. The protocol locking while crabbing goes 21.____
    A. down the tree and back up   B. up the tree and back down
    C. down the tree and releases   D. up the tree and releases

22. To reduce overhead and retrieve records from storage we use 22.____
    A. logs   B. log buffer
    C. medieval space   D. lower records

23. The space on disk allocated by the operating system for storing virtual-memory pages are called 23.____
    A. latches   B. swap space
    C. dirty block   D. none of the above

24. In two-factor authentication, the users can face an attack called   24.____
    A. radiant   B. cross attack
    C. scripting   D. man-in-the-middle

25. The attack that force an application to execute an SQL query is called   25.____
    A. SQL injection   B. SQL   C. direct   D. application

KEY (CORRECT ANSWERS)

1.	A		11.	B
2.	B		12.	A
3.	B		13.	A
4.	B		14.	C
5.	B		15.	A
6.	A		16.	D
7.	D		17.	A
8.	B		18.	B
9.	C		19.	D
10.	B		20.	C

21.	A
22.	B
23.	B
24.	D
25.	A

EXAMINATION SECTION
TEST 1

DIRECTIONS: Each question or incomplete statement is followed by several suggested answers or completions. Select the one that BEST answers the question or completes the statement. *PRINT THE LETTER OF THE CORRECT ANSWER IN THE SPACE AT THE RIGHT.*

1. A database management system is   1.____

    A. hardware that monitors user log-ons and log-offs
    B. software that merges data into one pool
    C. firmware that allows high level languages to be used
    D. ROM used to store data
    E. RAM used to store data

2. A database manager   2.____

    A. is a software package
    B. is a collection of related files
    C. permits data to be easily retrieved and manipulated
    D. permits data to be easily stored
    E. all of the above

3. A specific advantage of a database management system is   3.____

    A. consolidation of files
    B. program dependence
    C. making programming harder
    D. restricting data flexibility
    E. all of the above

4. Which of the following is NOT an advantage of a database management system?   4.____

    A. Easing program maintenance
    B. Restricting data flexibility
    C. Providing data security
    D. Restricting data accessibility
    E. All of the above are advantages

5. One of the advantages of a database management system is   5.____

    A. standardization of program names
    B. standardization of paragraph names
    C. standardization of screen formats
    D. standardization of data names
    E. all are advantages of a database management system

6. A database management system promotes   6.____

    A. data distribution   B. program distribution
    C. data security   D. special situation values
    E. access distribution

7. Which of the following is NOT a type of database?　　　　7.____

    A. Network
    B. Flat file
    C. Relational
    D. Hierarchical
    E. All are types of databases

8. In a hierarchical database management system,　　　　8.____

    A. one data set is subservient to another
    B. a data set can be subservient to two or more other data sets
    C. data sets can be viewed as two-dimensional tables
    D. child data sets govern two or more parent data sets
    E. child data sets govern a single parent data set

9. In a network database management system,　　　　9.____

    A. one data set is subservient to another
    B. a data set can be subservient to two or more other data sets
    C. data sets can be viewed as two-dimensional tables
    D. child data sets govern two or more parent data sets
    E. child data sets govern a single parent data set

10. In a relational database management system,　　　　10.____

    A. one data set is subservient to another
    B. a data set can be subservient to two or more other data sets
    C. data sets can be viewed as two-dimensional tables
    D. child data sets govern two or more parent data sets
    E. child data sets govern a single parent data set

11. In a hierarchical database management system, a parent data set can govern how many other data sets?　　　　11.____

    A. 1　　　　B. 2　　　　C. 3
    D. 4　　　　E. All of the above

12. In a hierarchical database management system, a child data set is subservient to how many parent data sets?　　　　12.____

    A. 1　　　　B. 2　　　　C. 3
    D. 4　　　　E. All of the above

13. In a network database management system, a child data set is subservient to how many parent data sets?　　　　13.____

    A. 1　　　　B. 2　　　　C. 3
    D. 4　　　　E. All of the above

14. In a network database management system, a parent data set can govern how many other data sets?　　　　14.____

    A. 1　　　　B. 2　　　　C. 3
    D. 4　　　　E. All of the above

15. Which of the following database management systems is classified as relational? 15.____

    A. SQL   B. IMAGE   C. DDL   D. DML   E. IMS

16. Which of the following database management systems is classified as network? 16.____

    A. SQL   B. IMAGE   C. DDL   D. DML   E. IMS

17. Which of the following database management systems is classified as hierarchical? 17.____

    A. SQL   B. IMAGE   C. DDL   D. DML   E. IMS

18. In a relational database management system, a record is called a(n) 18.____

    A. relation   B. attribute   C. tuple
    D. join   E. none of the above

19. In a relational database management system, a file is called a(n) 19.____

    A. relation   B. attribute   C. tuple
    D. join   E. none of the above

20. In a relational database management system, a field is called a(n) 20.____

    A. relation   B. domain   C. tuple
    D. join   E. none of the above

KEY (CORRECT ANSWERS)

1.	B		11.	E
2.	E		12.	A
3.	A		13.	E
4.	B		14.	E
5.	D		15.	A
6.	C		16.	B
7.	B		17.	E
8.	A		18.	C
9.	B		19.	A
10.	C		20.	B

TEST 2

Each question or incomplete statement is followed by several suggested answers or completions. Select the one that BEST answers the question or completes the statement. *PRINT THE LETTER OF THE CORRECT ANSWER IN THE SPACE AT THE RIGHT.*

1. Which of the following is NOT a basic operation for a relational database management system?   1.____

    A. Delete a table   B. Create a table
    C. Join a table   D. Union a table
    E. Delete a tuple

2. A database management system that contains its own language for manipulating the database management system is called   2.____

    A. self-contained   B. host language
    C. network   D. QUERY
    E. relational

3. A database management system that uses a high level language like COBOL to manipulate the database management system is called   3.____

    A. self-contained   B. host language
    C. network   D. QUERY
    E. relational

4. Which of the following is a language designed for novice users to locate and retrieve data?   4.____

    A. IMS   B. DDL   C. QUERY   D. COBOL   E. Pascal

5. Which of the following is NOT a common database management system utility routine?   5.____

    A. Initialization   B. Copying
    C. Capacity changes   D. Transaction logging
    E. None of the above

6. Generally given credit for development of relational database management systems is   6.____

    A. Grace Hopper   B. Ada Lovelace
    C. Blaise Pascal   D. Edgar Codd
    E. Warnier Orr

7. Relational database management systems were developed in the   7.____

    A. 1950's   B. 1960's   C. 1970's   D. 1980's   E. 1940's

8. Relational database management system can be found on _____ computers.   8.____

    A. personal   B. main frame   C. mini
    D. hobby   E. all types of

9. Which of the following relational operations means to combine relations?   9.____

    A. Copy   B. Print   C. Create
    D. Join   E. Add an attribute

10. We define a database management system with a

    A. DML   B. COBOL program   C. schema or DDL
    D. IMS   E. QUERY

10.____

11. We can read, store, or modify data in a database management system with a(n)

    A. DML   B. COBOL program   C. schema or DDL
    D. IMS   E. QUERY

11.____

12. A novice user can interrogate a database management system with

    A. DML   B. COBOL program   C. schema or DDL
    D. IMS   E. QUERY

12.____

13. A commonly used database management system is

    A. DML   B. COBOL program   C. schema or DDL
    D. IMS   E. QUERY

13.____

14. Which of the following is NOT an example of a database management system control system?

    A. Transaction logging   B. Checking access rights
    C. Back down   D. Back up
    E. All are control systems

14.____

15. Which of the following database management system control system records all changes made to the database management system?

    A. Transaction logging   B. Checking access rights
    C. Back down   D. Back up
    E. All are control systems

15.____

16. Which of the following database management system control systems tests for read or write capability?

    A. Transaction logging   B. Checking access rights
    C. Back down   D. Back up
    E. All are control systems

16.____

17. Which of the following database management system control systems copies the database management system to another disk or tape?

    A. Transaction logging   B. Checking access rights
    C. Back down   D. Back up
    E. All are control systems

17.____

18. IMAGE is a

    A. network database management system
    B. operation on Hewlett Packard computers
    C. system that has an Inquiry language called QUERY
    D. host language system
    E. All of the above

18.____

19. IBM's IMS   19.____

    A. is a network database management system
    B. operates on Hewlett Packard computers
    C. has an Inquiry language called QUERY
    D. is a host language system
    E. is none of the above

20. Burroughs DMS-II   20.____

    A. is a network database management system
    B. operates on Hewlett Packard computers
    C. has an Inquiry language called QUERY
    D. is a host language system
    E. is all of the above

_____

KEY (CORRECT ANSWERS)

1.	D	11.	B
2.	A	12.	E
3.	B	13.	D
4.	C	14.	C
5.	E	15.	A
6.	D	16.	B
7.	C	17.	D
8.	E	18.	E
9.	D	19.	E
10.	C	20.	A

_____

EXAMINATION SECTION
TEST 1

DIRECTIONS: Each question or incomplete statement is followed by several suggested answers or completions. Select the one that BEST answers the question or completes the statement. *PRINT THE LETTER OF THE CORRECT ANSWER IN THE SPACE AT THE RIGHT.*

1. The maintenance and use of computer hardware is assigned to the _____ group in the data processing department.   1.____

    A.   systems   B.   programming   C.   database
    D.   analysis   E.   operations

2. The equipment which makes up a computer system is called   2.____

    A.   hardcopy   B.   software
    C.   CPU   D.   peripheral devices
    E.   hardware

3. The entering of data into a computer system is the responsibility of the   3.____

    A.   programmers   B.   analysts
    C.   data control clerk   D.   data entry clerk
    E.   computer operator

4. The MOST common input media is(are) the   4.____

    A.   sound cards   B.   magnetic tape
    C.   magnetic disk   D.   compact disk
    E.   keyboard

5. The coding, testing, and debugging of computer software is the duty of the   5.____

    A.   programmer   B.   analyst
    C.   operator   D.   data control clerk
    E.   data entry clerk

6. _____ is the term associated with the off-line preparation of data later submitted for processing with other data that has been prepared off-line.   6.____

    A.   Timesharing   B.   Batch processing
    C.   Interactive processing   D.   Real-time processing
    E.   Aggregate processing

7. Multiple users share a single computer's resources in   7.____

    A.   batch processing   B.   interactive processing
    C.   microprocessing   D.   timesharing
    E.   all of the above

8. The _____ field is the LARGEST consumer of computer products and services.   8.____

    A.   science   B.   business   C.   health
    D.   military   E.   education

9. The _____ is considered to be an end-user of computer services.   9.___

    A. accountant   B. programmer
    C. operator   D. analyst
    E. database administrator

10. In the organization of data, a group of related fields that pertains to a single data entity is   10.___
    called a

    A. character   B. record   C. file
    D. database   E. key field

11. A _____ field uniquely identifies a record in a file.   11.___

    A. descriptive   B. indicative   C. normal key
    D. key   E. none of the above

12. A collection of records within the SAME classification is called a   12.___

    A. character   B. database   C. field
    D. record   E. none of the above

13. The CORRECT hierarchy of data is   13.___

    A. character, field, file, record
    B. character, file, record, field
    C. field, record, file, database
    D. character, field, record, file, database
    E. database, file, record, character, field

14. Which of the following data items located on a record would be BEST suited as a key   14.___
    field?

    A. Hours worked   B. Rate of pay
    C. Social security number   D. First name
    E. Last name

15. An example of a logic function is determining that   15.___

    A. 10 is 3 more than 7
    B. 12 plus 6 is 18
    C. 11 is an odd number
    D. 10 is not equal to 20
    E. all of the above

16. Which of the following is an example of a logic function performed by the computer?   16.___

    A. Determining that 60 is an even number
    B. Knowing that 120 is 12 dozen
    C. Arranging a group of numbers in ascending sequence
    D. Determining that 15 is 8 more than 7
    E. Determining that 12 minus 7 is 5

17. Which of the following is an arithmetic process performed by the computer?   17.___

    A. Arranging a group of numbers in descending order
    B. Arranging a group of numbers in ascending order

C. Determining that 5 plus 4 is 9
D. Knowing that 6 is an even number
E. All of the above

18. An example of numeric data is   18.____

   A. 3
   B. THREE
   C. $300.45
   D. three hundred dollars forty-five cents
   E. none of the above

19. A coding technique used by banks to process checks is   19.____

   A. OCR   B. UPC   C. MICR
   D. Hollerith   E. SQL

20. The duplicate copy of an existing file is a(an) _____ file.   20.____

   A. duplicate   B. grandfather   C. backup
   D. archive   E. save

21. _____ code is used for the internal storage of data in the computer. 21.____

   A. ASCII   B. EBCDIC   C. Binary
   D. Packed decimal   E. All of the above

22. An example of a peripheral device is the   22.____

   A. CPU   B. ALU   C. control unit
   D. disk drive   E. memory

23. The part of the computer that performs logical and arithmetic functions is the 23.____

   A. memory   B. control unit   C. disk
   D. ALU   E. CPU

24. Of the following, the secondary storage media that offers the FASTEST data storage and 24.____
    retrieval is the

   A. computer memory   B. floppy disk
   C. magnetic disk   D. zip drive
   E. digital tape

25. An example of an input/output device is the   25.____

   A. magnetic tape   B. magnetic disk
   C. CPU   D. disk drive
   E. all of the above

KEY (CORRECT ANSWERS)

1.	E		11.	D
2.	E		12.	E
3.	D		13.	D
4.	C		14.	C
5.	A		15.	D
6.	B		16.	C
7.	D		17.	C
8.	B		18.	A
9.	A		19.	C
10.	B		20.	C

21.	E
22.	D
23.	D
24.	C
25.	D

———

TEST 2

DIRECTIONS: Each question or incomplete statement is followed by several suggested answers or completions. Select the one that BEST answers the question or completes the statement. *PRINT THE LETTER OF THE CORRECT ANSWER IN THE SPACE AT THE RIGHT.*

1. The computerized retrieval of microfilm is referred to as

    A. OCR   B. COM   C. microfax
    D. MICR   E. CAD/CAM

    1.____

2. The _____ is a very high speed non-impact printer.

    A. daisy wheel   B. chain printer
    C. laser printer   D. plotter
    E. dot-matrix printer

    2.____

3. A computer which inputs data from physical measurements such as heat, motion, or touch is called a _____ computer.

    A. digital   B. analog   C. mainframe
    D. micro   E. mini

    3.____

4. A _____ computer performs general purpose, multiple concurrent operations with many users.

    A. micro   B. mini   C. mainframe
    D. timesharing   E. All of the above

    4.____

5. Some smaller computers are comparable to larger computers in performance, but are considered to be *task-oriented.* They may handle multiple users, but they primarily work on a single type of application such as accounting, billing, or inventory.
   This paragraph BEST describes _____ computers.

    A. mainframe   B. micro   C. mini
    D. super   E. general purpose

    5.____

6. The MOST widely used computer language is

    A. Cobol   B. Pascal   C. RPG
    D. Fortran   E. Basic

    6.____

7. The software which converts a high-level language like Fortran into the machine language which is directly understood by the computer is called a(n)

    A. preprocessor   B. multiplexor
    C. source originator   D. compiler
    E. all of the above

    7.____

8. _____ is NOT a *high-level* computer language.

    A. Cobol   B. Basic   C. RPG
    D. PL/1   E. Assembler

    8.____

9. _____ is used PRIMARILY in the scientific and engineering community.

    A. Cobol   B. Basic   C. Machine language
    D. PL/1   E. Fortran

    9.____

10. An example of a computer language used effectively for business applications is   10.___

    A. Cobol   B. RPG   C. Basic
    D. PL/1   E. all of the above

11. Which of the following terms is CLOSELY associated with the term *structured program-*   11.___
ming?

    A. HIPO   B. Top-down design
    C. Hierarchy chart   D. Modular programming
    E. All of the above

12. A storage capacity of 640K is APPROXIMATELY _____ bytes.   12.___

    A. 640,000,000   B. 64,000   C. 640,000
    D. 6,400,000   E. 640

13. A computer disk is divided into concentric circles called   13.___

    A. tracks   B. cylinders   C. rings
    D. sectors   E. segments

14. In order to ensure the accuracy of data stored on tape or disk, the computer will append   14.___
a _____ to each byte of data.

    A. check digit   B. parity bit   C. check bit
    D. modula 11 bit   E. validation bit

15. Direct access is a feature of the   15.___

    A. magnetic tape   B. memory card
    C. magnetic disk   D. compiler
    E. none of the above

16. When used, magnetic tape is BEST suited for situations where   16.___

    A. data is accessed sequentially
    B. VSAM is the data access method
    C. ISAM is the data access method
    D. data is accessed using direct access
    E. KSAM is the data access method

17. A term used to describe the algorithmic process of converting a key field into a storage   17.___
location is

    A. hashing   B. ISAM   C. VSAM
    D. indexing   E. dynamic storage

18. The software which controls the general operating procedures of the computer is the   18.___

    A. applications program   B. source program
    C. object program   D. operating system
    E. systems program

19. The computer language used to DIRECTLY communicate with the computer's operating   19.___
software is

    A. RPG   B. DOS   C. JCL
    D. VSAM   E. none of the above

20. A common pathway on which all data travels to and from the CPU to peripheral devices is the 20.____

    A. channel   B. line   C. bus
    D. modem   E. multiplexor

21. The _____ converts computer signals to be transferred over telephone lines and vice versa. 21.____

    A. coaxial cable   B. multiplexor
    C. modem   D. controller
    E. digital teleprocessor

22. *Baud* is a measurement of 22.____

    A. storage capacity   B. CPU performance
    C. disk speed   D. printer speed
    E. transmission speed

23. _____ is a type of network COMMONLY used on micro-computers. 23.____

    A. Narrowband   B. LAN   C. Star
    D. Ring   E. Hub

24. A type of computer that will handle the preliminary processing of data BEFORE it is sent to the mainframe computer is called a 24.____

    A. pre-processor   B. front-end processor
    C. back-end processor   D. minicomputer
    E. slave computer

25. The _____ would NOT be a member of the data processing staff in an organization. 25.____

    A. analyst   B. programmer   C. auditor
    D. operator   E. data entry clerk

KEY (CORRECT ANSWERS)

1.	B		11.	E
2.	C		12.	C
3.	B		13.	B
4.	C		14.	B
5.	C		15.	C
6.	A		16.	A
7.	D		17.	A
8.	E		18.	D
9.	E		19.	C
10.	E		20.	C

21. C
22. E
23. B
24. B
25. C

—————

EXAMINATION SECTION
TEST 1

DIRECTIONS: Each question or incomplete statement is followed by several suggested answers or completions. Select the one that BEST answers the question or completes the statement. *PRINT THE LETTER OF THE CORRECT ANSWER IN THE SPACE AT THE RIGHT.*

1. Which of the following words in a pseudocode statement can be replaced by the word *read?*   1.____

   A. Get   B. Print   C. Set   D. Store

2. Units of input and output in pseudocode are known as   2.____

   A. lines   B. items   C. strings   D. records

3. The statement required to print the value of number of students followed by the label PEOPLE would be written: 3.____

   A. Set value to *PEOPLE*
   B. Print *number of students* and *PEOPLE*
   C. Read number of students and *PEOPLE*
   D. Write number of students and *PEOPLE*

4. What command word is used to save contents of another storage location or a constant in a storage location?   4.____

   A. Store   B. Set   C. Get   D. Put

5. The symbol used for multiplication in pseudocode is   5.____

   A.   B. /   C. *   D. x

6. A statement constructed to give the first number in a data set the same value as the second number would be expressed as _____ first number _____ second number.   6.____

   A. read; as   B. set; to
   C. declare; as   D. —; =

7. The function of a literal is to   7.____

   A. read stored values
   B. identify or describe output
   C. write results
   D. store input values

8. What is the term for a grouping of items that have a similar characteristic or common identifying property?   8.____

   A. Set   B. Array
   C. String   D. Assortment

9. When calculations are written in algebraic expression, the name of the storage location in which the result would be *save* is expressed as   9.____

   A. zero   B. =   C. x   D. y

10. If a value of 10 is stored in memory at X, the output that the statement *Print 'X'* would produce is

    A. 10   B. 'X'   C. X   D. X = 10

10.____

11. Which of the following steps in using a subprogram would occur FIRST?

    A. Subprogram executed
    B. Subprogram invoked
    C. Program continues execution
    D. Results passed through program

11.____

12. A declaration for the data item *inventory item stock number* would be written: Declare

    A. stock number, numeric inventory item
    B. numeric inventory item stock number
    C. inventory item stock number
    D. character inventory item stock number

12.____

13. Of the following, a(n) _____ is NOT always an element of the *loop while* construct.

    A. *end loop* statement
    B. counter
    C. group of one or more statements forming the loop body
    D. means of making the *loop while* condition false

13.____

14. Information is placed into a storage location by means of a(n) _____ statement.

    A. call   B. assignment
    C. return   D. address

14.____

15. A programmer wants to place a zero into a memory location that is to contain a counter. Each of the following is a possible statement EXCEPT:

    A. Set counter to zero
    B. Initialize zero in counter
    C. Set COUNT to zero
    D. Store zero in counter

15.____

16. What is the term used for the items of information necessary for a program or subprogram to perform its task?

    A. Records   B. Functions
    C. Parameters   D. Constructs

16.____

17. Which of the following items of input would be needed in order to construct a module that finds the sum of two arrays, A and B?
The

    A. number of elements in A and B
    B. loop for J = 1 to the number of elements in A and B
    C. two numbers, J and K
    D. sum of the two arrays

17.____

18. A statement constructed to initialize a total cost at zero would be written: 18.____

    A. Set total cost to zero   B. Set zero to total cost
    C. Total cost =0   D. Read total cost as zero

19. In order to provide a means of executing a named block of statements, the _____ is   19.____
used.

    A. call statement   B. selection parameter
    C. return statement   D. do module

20. Each element in an array is identified by a number called a _____ , which designates   20.____
position in the array.

    A. marker   B. literal
    C. string   D. subscript

21. A value of 8 is stored in memory at X.   21.____
The following statement would produce the output X = 8.

    A. Print X = 8   B. Read X as 8
    C. Print 'X =' and X   D. Print 'X = 8'

22. The symbol for division in pseudocode is   22.____

    A. —   B. ∫   C. ÷   D. /

23. A data item is denoted as non-numeric by means of a(n)   23.____

    A. record   B. string   C. address   D. name

24. A statement constructed to set the value of an employee count to zero would be written: 24.____

    A. Get zero employee count
    B. Read zero for employee count
    C. Set employee count to zero
    D. Put employee count at zero

25. Which of the following key words is NOT used for the purpose of selection in   25.____
pseudocode?

    A. Else   B. Then   C. While   D. If

KEY (CORRECT ANSWERS)

1.	A		11.	B
2.	D		12.	D
3.	D		13.	B
4.	B		14.	B
5.	C		15.	B
6.	B		16.	C
7.	B		17.	A
8.	B		18.	A
9.	C		19.	D
10.	C		20.	D

21.	C
22.	D
23.	B
24.	C
25.	C

TEST 2

DIRECTIONS: Each question or incomplete statement is followed by several suggested answers or completions. Select the one that BEST answers the question or completes the statement. *PRINT THE LETTER OF THE CORRECT ANSWER IN THE SPACE AT THE RIGHT.*

1. To perform loop operation, each of the following must be done to the counter EXCEPT   1.____

   A. division   B. initialization
   C. testing   D. incrementation

2. A subprogram that finds the largest element in an array can be constructed as a   2.____

   A. loop   B. function
   C. loop with counter   D. do module

3. *Read employee's name, hourly pay rate, number of hours worked, and gross pay.*   3.____
   In the above statement, the optional word is

   A. rate   B. and   C. number   D. read

4. *Find degrees Fahrenheit by multiplying degrees centigrade by nine-fifths and adding 32*   4.____
   to the result.
   To compute and save the result for the above, the required statement using algebraic
   form would be written:

   A. F = ((9*C)/5) + 32
   B. F = (9/5)xC) + 32
   C. Set F to ((9.C/5) + 32
   D. F = 9/5C + 32

5. Output in pseudocode is indicated by each of the following key words EXCEPT   5.____

   A. print   B. get   C. write   D. put

6. The _____ statement is placed at the bottom of a selection group.   6.____

   A. call   B. return   C. do   D. end if

7. A statement constructed to save 100 in number of people would be written: 7.____

   A. Read 100 for number of people
   B. Store 100 for number of people
   C. Set 100 for number of people
   D. Set number of people to 100

8. In pseudocode, the *loop with counter* construct is specified by the key words   8.____

   A. loop while   B. end loop
   C. loop for   D. end if

9. A programmer wishes to construct a nested selection to handle the following case: Add 1   9.____
   to senior resident counter when town residence is Oakville and person's age is greater
   than 64.
   In the best logical construction, the statement would begin:

A. Others counter = others counter + 1
B. If town of residence is Oakville
C. If age is greater than 64
D. Senior residence counter = senior resident counter + 1

10. Which of the following terms is NOT used to indicate the meaning of output in pseudocode?   10.____

    A. Character string   B. Label
    C. Record   D. Literal

11. What kind of statement is used to revert control to a calling program?   11.____

    A. Call   B. End loop
    C. Return   D. Reassignment

12. The statement required to save the literal SUSPENDED in student status would be written: 12.____

    A. Write student status as SUSPENDED
    B. Get SUSPENDED to student status
    C. Set student status to 'SUSPENDED'
    D. Read student status as 'SUSPENDED'

13. Which of the following words in a pseudocode statement can be replaced by the word *print*?   13.____

    A. Get   B. Print   C. Set   D. Store

14. In pseudocode, the = symbol indicates   14.____

    A. division
    B. an equality of values
    C. a read command
    D. a storage assignment for information

15. Which of the following steps in using a subprogram would occur LAST?   15.____

    A. Subprogram executed
    B. Subprogram invoked
    C. Program continues execution
    D. Results passed through program

16. If a value of 10 is stored in memory at X, the statement *Print X* will produce the output   16.____

    A. 10   B. 'X'   C. X   D. X = 10

17. Which of the following is NOT an example of a non-numeric data item?   17.____

    A. Telephone number
    B. ZIP code
    C. Student identification number
    D. Temperature

18. For moving the contents of one storage location to another location in algebraic expression, a statement of the form _____ should be used.   18.____

   A. x = y   B. Move x to y
   C. x/y   D. Set x to y

19. A declaration for the data item *number of employees* would be written: Declare   19.____

   A. employees, number of
   B. numeric number of employees
   C. number of employees
   D. character number of employees

20. In a *loop while* construct, the loop will be terminated upon the introduction of a(n)   20.____

   A. false condition   B. return statement
   C. subprogram   D. *end if* statement

21. The statement required to print the message GROSS PAY IS $ followed by the value of gross pay would be written: 21.____

   A. Get gross pay and GROSS PAY IS $
   B. Read 'GROSS PAY IS $' and gross pay
   C. Write 'GROSS PAY IS $' and gross pay
   D. Print 'GROSS PAY IS $' and gross pay

22. In pseudocode, the value x^2 would be written   22.____

   A. X-2   B. X**2   C. X//2   D. X*2

23. A statement using algebraic form to compute and save the result for *Add one to number of days* would be written: 23.____

   A. Number of days + 1
   B. Number of days = number of days + 1
   C. Set number of days to number of days + 1
   D. Set number of days + 1

24. What type of statement is used to invoke a subprogram?   24.____

   A. Do   B. Call
   C. Assignment   D. Return

25. A programmer wants to construct a statement that instructs the computer to print the message *There is no sales tax* if the tax code is zero and *The sales tax is 4%* otherwise. In the statement, what would follow the key word *else?*   25.____

   A. Write 'There is no sales tax'
   B. Get tax code
   C. Write 'The sales tax is 4%'
   D. Set tax code to zero

KEY (CORRECT ANSWERS)

1.	A		11.	C
2.	B		12.	C
3.	B		13.	B
4.	A		14.	D
5.	B		15.	C
6.	D		16.	A
7.	D		17.	D
8.	C		18.	A
9.	C		19.	B
10.	C		20.	A

21.	C
22.	B
23.	B
24.	B
25.	C

———

GLOSSARY OF COMPUTER TERMS

Contents

GLOSSARY OF COMPUTER TERMS

Basic

application & app
An application (often called "app" for short) is simply a program with a GUI. Note that it is different from an applet.

boot
Starting up an OS is booting it. If the computer is already running, it is more often called rebooting.

browser
A browser is a program used to browse the web. Some common browsers include Netscape, MSIE (Microsoft Internet Explorer), Safari, Lynx, Mosaic, Amaya, Arena, Chimera, Opera, Cyberdog, HotJava, etc.

bug
A bug is a mistake in the design of something, especially software. A really severe bug can cause something to crash.

chat
Chatting is like e-mail, only it is done instantaneously and can directly involve multiple people at once. While e-mail now relies on one more or less standard protocol, chatting still has a couple competing ones. Of particular note are IRC and Instant Messenger. One step beyond chatting is called MUDding.

click
To press a mouse button. When done twice in rapid succession, it is referred to as a double-click.

cursor
A point of attention on the computer screen, often marked with a flashing line or block. Text typed into the computer will usually appear at the cursor.

database
A database is a collection of data, typically organized to make common retrievals easy and efficient. Some common database programs include Oracle, Sybase, Postgres, Informix, Filemaker, Adabas, etc.

desktop
A desktop system is a computer designed to sit in one position on a desk somewhere and not move around. Most general purpose computers are desktop systems. Calling a system a desktop implies nothing about its platform. The fastest desktop system at any given time is typically either an Alpha or PowerPC based system, but the SPARC and PA-RISC based systems are also often in the running. Industrial strength desktops are typically called workstations.

directory
Also called "folder", a directory is a collection of files typically created for organizational purposes. Note that a directory is itself a file, so a directory can generally contain other directories. It differs in this way from a partition.

disk
A disk is a physical object used for storing data. It will not forget its data when it loses power. It is always used in conjunction with a disk drive. Some disks can be removed from their drives, some cannot. Generally it is possible to write new information to a disk in addition to reading data from it, but this is not always the case.

drive

A device for storing and/or retrieving data. Some drives (such as disk drives, zip drives, and tape drives) are typically capable of having new data written to them, but some others (like CD-ROMs or DVD-ROMs) are not. Some drives have random access (like disk drives, zip drives, CD-ROMs, and DVD-ROMs), while others only have sequential access (like tape drives).

e-book

The concept behind an e-book is that it should provide all the functionality of an ordinary book but in a manner that is (overall) less expensive and more environmentally friendly. The actual term e-book is somewhat confusingly used to refer to a variety of things: custom software to play e-book titles, dedicated hardware to play e-book titles, and the e-book titles themselves. Individual e-book titles can be free or commercial (but will always be less expensive than their printed counterparts) and have to be loaded into a player to be read. Players vary wildly in capability level. Basic ones allow simple reading and bookmarking; better ones include various features like hypertext, illustrations, audio, and even limited video. Other optional features allow the user to mark-up sections of text, leave notes, circle or diagram things, highlight passages, program or customize settings, and even use interactive fiction. There are many types of e-book; a couple popular ones include the Newton book and Palm DOC.

e-mail

E-mail is short for electronic mail. It allows for the transfer of information from one computer to another, provided that they are hooked up via some sort of network (often the Internet. E-mail works similarly to FAXing, but its contents typically get printed out on the other end only on demand, not immediately and automatically as with FAX. A machine receiving e-mail will also not reject other incoming mail messages as a busy FAX machine will; rather they will instead be queued up to be received after the current batch has been completed. E-mail is only seven-bit clean, meaning that you should not expect anything other than ASCII data to go through uncorrupted without prior conversion via something like uucode or bcode. Some mailers will do some conversion automatically, but unless you know your mailer is one of them, you may want to do the encoding manually.

file

A file is a unit of (usually named) information stored on a computer.

firmware

Sort of in-between hardware and software, firmware consists of modifiable programs embedded in hardware. Firmware updates should be treated with care since they can literally destroy the underlying hardare if done improperly. There are also cases where neglecting to apply a firmware update can destroy the underlying hardware, so user beware.

floppy

An extremely common type of removable disk. Floppies do not hold too much data, but most computers are capable of reading them. Note though that there are different competing format used for floppies, so that a floppy written by one type of computer might not directly work on another. Also sometimes called "diskette".

format

The manner in which data is stored; its organization. For example, VHS, SVHS, and Beta are three different formats of video tape. They are not 100% compatible with each other, but information can be transferred from one to the other with the proper equipment (but not always without loss; SVHS contains more information than either of the other two). Computer information can be stored in literally hundreds of different formats, and can represent text, sounds, graphics, animations, etc. Computer information can be exchanged via different computer types provided both computers can interpret the format used.

function keys

On a computer keyboard, the keys that start with an "F" that are usually (but not always) found on the top row. They are meant to perform user-defined tasks.

graphics

Anything visually displayed on a computer that is not text.

hardware

The physical portion of the computer.

hypertext

A hypertext document is like a text document with the ability to contain pointers to other regions of (possibly other) hypertext documents.

Internet

The Internet is the world-wide network of computers. There is only one Internet, and thus it is typically capitalized (although it is sometimes referred to as "the 'net"). It is different from an intranet.

keyboard

A keyboard on a computer is almost identical to a keyboard on a typewriter. Computer keyboards will typically have extra keys, however. Some of these keys (common examples include Control, Alt, and Meta) are meant to be used in conjunction with other keys just like shift on a regular typewriter. Other keys (common examples include Insert, Delete, Home, End, Help, function keys,etc.) are meant to be used independently and often perform editing tasks. Keyboards on different platforms will often look slightly different and have somewhat different collections of keys. Some keyboards even have independent shift lock and caps lock keys. Smaller keyboards with only math-related keys are typically called "keypads".

language

Computer programs can be written in a variety of different languages. Different languages are optimized for different tasks. Common languages include Java, C, C++, ForTran, Pascal, Lisp, and BASIC. Some people classify languages into two categories, higher-level and lower-level. These people would consider assembly language and machine language lower-level languages and all other languages higher-level. In general, higher-level languages can be either interpreted or compiled; many languages allow both, but some are restricted to one or the other. Many people do not consider machine language and assembly language at all when talking about programming languages.

laptop

A laptop is any computer designed to do pretty much anything a desktop system can do but run for a short time (usually two to five hours) on batteries. They are designed to be carried around but are not particularly convenient to carry around. They are significantly more expensive than desktop systems and have far worse battery life than PDAs. Calling a system a laptop implies nothing about its platform. By far the fastest laptops are the PowerPC based Macintoshes.

memory

Computer memory is used to temporarily store data. In reality, computer memory is only capable of remembering sequences of zeros and ones, but by utilizing the binary number system it is possible to produce arbitrary rational numbers and through clever formatting all manner of representations of pictures, sounds, and animations. The most common types of memory are RAM, ROM, and flash.

MHz & megahertz

One megahertz is equivalent to 1000 kilohertz, or 1,000,000 hertz. The clock speed of the main processor of many computers is measured in MHz, and is sometimes (quite misleadingly) used to represent the overall speed of a computer. In fact, a computer's speed is based upon many factors, and since MHz only reveals how many clock cycles the main processor has per second (saying nothing about how much is actually accomplished per cycle), it can really only accurately be used to gauge two computers with the same generation and family of processor plus similar configurations of memory, co-processors, and other peripheral hardware.

modem

A modem allows two computers to communicate over ordinary phone lines. It derives its name from **mod**ulate / **dem**odulate, the process by which it converts digital computer data back and forth for use with an analog phone line.

monitor

The screen for viewing computer information is called a monitor.

mouse

In computer parlance a mouse can be both the physical object moved around to control a pointer on the screen, and the pointer itself. Unlike the animal, the proper plural of computer mouse is "mouses".

multimedia

This originally indicated a capability to work with and integrate various types of things including audio, still graphics, and especially video. Now it is more of a marketing term and has little real meaning. Historically the Amiga was the first multimedia machine. Today in addition to AmigaOS, IRIX and Solaris are popular choices for high-end multimedia work.

NC

The term **n**etwork **c**omputer refers to any (usually desktop) computer system that is designed to work as part of a network rather than as a stand-alone machine. This saves money on hardware, software, and maintenance by taking advantage of facilities already available on the network. The term "Internet appliance" is often used interchangeably with NC.

network

A network (as applied to computers) typically means a group of computers working together. It can also refer to the physical wire etc. connecting the computers.

notebook

A notebook is a small laptop with similar price, performance, and battery life.

organizer

An organizer is a tiny computer used primarily to store names, addresses, phone numbers, and date book information. They usually have some ability to exchange information with desktop systems. They boast even better battery life than PDAs but are far less capable. They are extremely inexpensive but are typically incapable of running any special purpose applications and are thus of limited use.

OS

The **o**perating **s**ystem is the program that manages a computer's resources. Common OSes include Windows '95, MacOS, Linux, Solaris, AmigaOS, AIX, Windows NT, etc.

PC

The term **p**ersonal **c**omputer properly refers to any desktop, laptop, or notebook computer system. Its use is inconsistent, though, and some use it to specifically refer to x86 based systems running MS-DOS, MS-Windows, GEOS, or OS/2. This latter use is similar to what is meant by a WinTel system.

PDA

A **p**ersonal **d**igital **a**ssistant is a small battery-powered computer intended to be carried around by the user rather than left on a desk. This means that the processor used ought to be power-efficient as well as fast, and the OS ought to be optimized for hand-held use. PDAs typically have an instant-on feature (they would be useless without it) and most are grayscale rather than color because of battery life issues. Most have a pen interface and come with a detachable stylus. None use mouses. All have some ability to exchange data with desktop systems. In terms of raw capabilities, a PDA is more capable than an organizer and less capable than a laptop (although some high-end PDAs beat out some low-end laptops). By far the most popular PDA is the Pilot, but other common types include Newtons, Psions, Zauri, Zoomers, and Windows CE hand-helds. By far the fastest current PDA is the Newton (based around a StrongARM RISC processor). Other PDAs are optimized for other tasks; few computers are as personal as PDAs and care must be taken in their purchase. Feneric's PDA / Handheld Comparison Page is perhaps the most detailed comparison of PDAs and handheld computers to be found anywhere on the web.

platform

Roughly speaking, a platform represents a computer's family. It is defined by both the processor type on the hardware side and the OS type on the software side. Computers belonging to different platforms cannot typically run each other's programs (unless the programs are written in a language like Java).

portable

If something is portable it can be easily moved from one type of computer to another. The verb "to port" indicates the moving itself.

printer

A printer is a piece of hardware that will print computer information onto paper.

processor

The processor (also called central processing unit, or CPU) is the part of the computer that actually works with the data and runs the programs. There are two main processor types in common usage today: CISC and RISC. Some computers have more than one processor and are thus called "multiprocessor". This is distinct from multitasking. Advertisers often use megahertz numbers as a means of showing a processor's speed. This is often extremely misleading; megahertz numbers are more or less meaningless when compared across different types of processors.

program

A program is a series of instructions for a computer, telling it what to do or how to behave. The terms "application" and "app" mean almost the same thing (albeit applications generally have GUIs). It is however different from an applet. Program is also the verb that means to create a program, and a programmer is one who programs.

run

Running a program is how it is made to do something. The term "execute" means the same thing.

software

The non-physical portion of the computer; the part that exists only as data; the programs. Another term meaning much the same is "code".

spreadsheet

An program used to perform various calculations. It is especially popular for financial applications. Some common spreadsheets include Lotus 123, Excel, OpenOffice Spreadsheet, Octave, Gnumeric, AppleWorks Spreadsheet, Oleo, and GeoCalc.

user

The operator of a computer.

word processor

A program designed to help with the production of textual documents, like letters and memos. Heavier duty work can be done with a desktop publisher. Some common word processors include MS-Word, OpenOffice Write, WordPerfect, AbiWord, AppleWorks Write, and GeoWrite.

www

The World-Wide-Web refers more or less to all the publically accessible documents on the Internet. It is used quite loosely, and sometimes indicates only HTML files and sometimes FTP and Gopher files, too. It is also sometimes just referred to as "the web".

Reference

65xx

The 65xx series of processors includes the 6502, 65C02, 6510, 8502, 65C816, 65C816S, etc. It is a CISC design and is not being used in too many new stand-alone computer systems, but is still being used in embedded systems, game systems (such as the Super NES), and processor enhancement add-ons for older systems. It was originally designed by MOS Technologies, but is now produced by The Western Design Center, Inc. It was the primary processor for many extremely popular systems no longer being produced, including the Commodore 64, the Commodore 128, and all the Apple][series machines.

68xx

The 68xx series of processors includes the 6800, 6805, 6809, 68000, 68020, 68030, 68040, 68060, etc. It is a CISC design and is not being used in too many new stand-alone computer systems, but is still being used heavily in embedded systems. It was originally designed by Motorola and was the primary processor for older generations of many current machines, including Macintoshes, Amigas, Sun workstations, HP workstations, etc. and the primary processor for many systems no longer being produced, such as the TRS-80. The PowerPC was designed in part to be its replacement.

a11y

Commonly used to abbreviate the word "accessibility". There are eleven letters between the "a" and the "y".

ADA

An object-oriented language at one point popular for military and some academic software. Lately C++ and Java have been getting more attention.

AI

Artificial intelligence is the concept of making computers do tasks once considered to require thinking. AI makes computers play chess, recognize handwriting and speech, helps suggest prescriptions to doctors for patients based on imput symptoms, and many other tasks, both mundane and not.

AIX

The industrial strength OS designed by IBM to run on PowerPC and x86 based machines. It is a variant of UNIX and is meant to provide more power than OS/2.

AJaX

AJaX is a little like DHTML, but it adds asynchronous communication between the browser and Web site via either XML or JSON to achieve performance that often rivals desktop applications.

Alpha

An Alpha is a RISC processor invented by Digital and currently produced by Digital/Compaq and Samsung. A few different OSes run on Alpha based machines including Digital UNIX, Windows NT, Linux, NetBSD, and AmigaOS. Historically, at any given time, the fastest processor in the world has usually been either an Alpha or a PowerPC (with sometimes SPARCs and PA-RISCs making the list), but Compaq has recently announced that there will be no further development of this superb processor instead banking on the release of the somewhat suspect Merced.

AltiVec

AltiVec (also called the "Velocity Engine") is a special extension built into some PowerPC CPUs to provide better performance for certain operations, most notably graphics and sound. It is similar to MMX on the x86 CPUs. Like MMX, it requires special software for full performance benefits to be realized.

Amiga

A platform originally created and only produced by Commodore, but now owned by Gateway 2000 and produced by it and a few smaller companies. It was historically the first multimedia machine and gave the world of computing many innovations. It is now primarily used for audio / video applications; in fact, a decent Amiga system is less expensive than a less capable video editing system. Many music videos were created on Amigas, and a few television series and movies had their special effects generated on Amigas. Also, Amigas can be readily synchronized with video cameras, so typically when a computer screen appears on television or in a movie and it is not flickering wildly, it is probably an Amiga in disguise. Furthermore, many coin-operated arcade games are really Amigas packaged in stand-up boxes. Amigas have AmigaOS for their OS. New Amigas have either a PowerPC or an Alpha for their main processor and a 68xx processor dedicated to graphics manipulation. Older (and low end) Amigas do everything with just a 68xx processor.

AmigaOS
The OS used by Amigas. AmigaOS combines the functionality of an OS and a window manager and is fully multitasking. AmigaOS boasts a pretty good selection of games (many arcade games are in fact written on Amigas) but has limited driver support. AmigaOS will run on 68xx, Alpha, and PowerPC based machines.

Apple][
The Apple][computer sold millions of units and is generally considered to have been the first home computer with a 1977 release date. It is based on the 65xx family of processors. The earlier Apple I was only available as a build-it-yourself kit.

AppleScript
A scripting language for Mac OS computers.

applet
An applet differs from an application in that is not meant to be run stand-alone but rather with the assistance of another program, usually a browser.

AppleTalk
AppleTalk is a protocol for computer networks. It is arguably inferior to TCP/IP.

Aqua
The default window manager for Mac OS X.

Archie
Archie is a system for searching through FTP archives for particular files. It tends not to be used too much anymore as more general modern search engines are significantly more capable.

ARM
An ARM is a RISC processor invented by Advanced RISC Machines, currently owned by Intel, and currently produced by both the above and Digital/Compaq. ARMs are different from most other processors in that they were not designed to maximize speed but rather to maximize speed per power consumed. Thus ARMs find most of their use on hand-held machines and PDAs. A few different OSes run on ARM based machines including Newton OS, JavaOS, and (soon) Windows CE and Linux. The StrongARM is a more recent design of the original ARM, and it is both faster and more power efficient than the original.

ASCII
The ASCII character set is the most popular one in common use. People will often refer to a bare text file without complicated embedded format instructions as an ASCII file, and such files can usually be transferred from one computer system to another with relative ease. Unfortunately there are a few minor variations of it that pop up here and there, and if you receive a text file that seems subtly messed up with punctuation marks altered or upper and lower case reversed, you are probably encountering one of the ASCII variants. It is usually fairly straightforward to translate from one ASCII variant to another, though. The ASCII character set is seven bit while pure binary is usually eight bit, so transferring a binary file through ASCII channels will result in corruption and loss of data. Note also that the ASCII character set is a

subset of the Unicode character set.

ASK

A protocol for an infrared communications port on a device. It predates the IrDA compliant infrared communications protocol and is not compatible with it. Many devices with infrared communications support both, but some only support one or the other.

assembly language

Assembly language is essentially machine language that has had some of the numbers replaced by somewhat easier to remember mnemonics in an attempt to make it more human-readable. The program that converts assembly language to machine language is called an assembler. While assembly language predates FORTRAN, it is not typically what people think of when they discuss computer languages.

Atom

Atom is an intended replacement for RSS and like it is used for syndicating a web site's content. It is currently not nearly as popular or well-supported by software applications, however.

authoring system

Any GUIs method of designing new software can be called an authoring system. Any computer language name with the word "visual" in front of it is probably a version of that language built with some authoring system capabilities. It appears that the first serious effort to produce a commercial quality authoring system took place in the mid eighties for the Amiga.

AWK

AWK is an interpreted language developed in 1977 by Aho, Weinberger, & Kernighan. It gets its name from its creators' initials. It is not particularly fast, but it was designed for creating small throwaway programs rather than full-blown applications -- it is designed to make the writing of the program fast, not the program itself. It is quite portable with versions existing for numerous platforms, including a free GNU version. Plus, virtually every version of UNIX in the world comes with AWK built-in.

BASIC

The Beginners' All-purpose Symbolic Instruction Code is a computer language developed by Kemeny & Kurtz in 1964. Although it is traditionally interpreted, compilers exist for many platforms. While the interpreted form is typically fairly slow, the compiled form is often quite fast, usually faster than Pascal. The biggest problem with BASIC is portability; versions for different machines are often completely unlike each other; Amiga BASIC at first glance looks more like Pascal, for example. Portability problems actually go beyond even the cross platform level; in fact, most machines have multiple versions of incompatible BASICs available for use. The most popular version of BASIC today is called Visual BASIC. Like all BASICs it has portability issues, but it has some of the advantages of an authoring system so it is relatively easy to use.

baud

A measure of communications speed, used typically for modems indicating how many bits per second can be transmitted.

BBS

A bulletin board system is a computer that can be directly connected to via modem and provides various services like e-mail, chatting, newsgroups, and file downloading. BBSs have waned in popularity as more and more people are instead connecting to the Internet, but they are still used for product support and local area access. Most current BBSs provide some sort of gateway connection to the Internet.

bcode

Identical in intent to uucode, bcode is slightly more efficient and more portable across different computer types. It is the preferred method used by MIME.

BeOS

A lightweight OS available for both PowerPC and x86 based machines. It is often referred to simply as "Be".

beta

A beta version of something is not yet ready for prime time but still possibly useful to related developers and other interested parties. Expect beta software to crash more than properly released software does. Traditionally beta versions (of commercial software) are distributed only to selected testers who are often then given a discount on the proper version after its release in exchange for their testing work. Beta versions of non-commercial software are more often freely available to anyone who has an interest.

binary

There are two meanings for binary in common computer usage. The first is the name of the number system in which there are only zeros and ones. This is important to computers because all computer data is ultimately a series of zeros and ones, and thus can be represented by binary numbers. The second is an offshoot of the first; data that is not meant to be intepreted through a common character set (like ASCII) is typically referred to as binary data. Pure binary data is typically eight bit data, and transferring a binary file through ASCII channels without prior modification will result in corruption and loss of data. Binary data can be turned into ASCII data via uucoding or bcoding.

bit

A bit can either be on or off; one or zero. All computer data can ultimately be reduced to a series of bits. The term is also used as a (very rough) measure of sound quality, color quality, and even procesor capability by considering the fact that series of bits can represent binary numbers. For example (without getting too technical), an eight bit image can contain at most 256 distinct colors while a sixteen bit image can contain at most 65,536 distinct colors.

bitmap

A bitmap is a simplistic representation of an image on a computer, simply indicating whether or not pixels are on or off, and sometimes indicating their color. Often fonts are represented as bitmaps. The term "pixmap" is sometimes used similarly; typically when a distinction is made, pixmap refers to color images and bitmap refers to monochrome images.

blog

Short for web log, a blog (or weblog, or less commonly, 'blog) is a web site containing periodic (usually frequent) posts. Blogs are usually syndicated via either some type of RSS or Atom and often supports TrackBacks. It is not uncommon for blogs to function much like newspaper columns. A blogger is someone who writes for and maintains a blog.

boolean

Boolean algebra is the mathematics of base two numbers. Since base two numbers have only two values, zero and one, there is a good analogy between base two numbers and the logical values "true" & "false". In common usage, booleans are therefore considered to be simple logical values like true & false and the operations that relate them, most typically "and", "or" and "not". Since everyone has a basic understanding of the concepts of true & false and basic conjunctions, everyone also has a basic understanding of boolean concepts -- they just may not realize it.

byte

A byte is a grouping of bits. It is typically eight bits, but there are those who use non-standard byte sizes. Bytes are usually measured in large groups, and the term "kilobyte" (often abbreviated as K) means one-thousand twenty-four (1024) bytes; the term "megabyte" (often abbreviated as M) means one-thousand twenty-four (1024) K; the term gigabyte (often abbreviated as G) means one-thousand twenty-four (1024) M; and the term "terabyte" (often abbreviated as T) means one-thousand twenty-four (1024) G. Memory is typically measured in kilobytes or megabytes, and disk space is typically measured in megabytes or gigabytes. Note that the multipliers here are 1024 instead of the more common 1000 as would be used in the metric system. This is to make it easier to work with the binary number system. Note also that some hardware manufacturers will use the smaller 1000 multiplier on M & G quantities to make their disk drives seem larger than they really are; buyer beware.

bytecode

Sometimes computer languages that are said to be either interpreted or compiled are in fact neither and are more accurately said to be somewhere in between. Such languages are compiled into bytecode which is then interpreted on the target system. Bytecode tends to be binary but will work on any machine with the appropriate runtime environment (or virtual machine) for it.

C

C is one of the most popular computer languages in the world, and quite possibly *the* most popular. It is a compiled langauge widely supported on many platforms. It tends to be more portable than FORTRAN but less portable than Java; it has been standardized by ANSI as "ANSI C" -- older versions are called either "K&R C" or "Kernighan and Ritchie C" (in honor of C's creators), or sometimes just "classic C". Fast and simple, it can be applied to all manner of general purpose tasks. C compilers are made by several companies, but the free GNU version (gcc) is still considered one of the best. Newer C-like object-oriented languages include both Java and C++.

C#

C# is a compiled object-oriented language based heavily on C++ with some Java features.

C++

C++ is a compiled object-oriented language. Based heavily on C, C++ is nearly as fast and can often be thought of as being just C with added features. It is currently probably the second most popular object-oriented language, but it has the drawback of being fairly complex -- the much simpler but somewhat slower Java is probably the most popular object-oriented language. Note that C++ was developed independently of the somewhat similar Objective-C; it is however related to Objective-C++.

C64/128

The Commodore 64 computer to this day holds the record for being the most successful model of computer ever made with even the lowest estimates being in the tens of millions. Its big brother, the Commodore 128, was not quite as popular but still sold several million units. Both units sported ROM-based BASIC and used it as a default "OS". The C128 also came with CP/M (it was a not-often-exercized option on the C64). In their later days they were also packaged with GEOS. Both are based on 65xx family processors. They are still in use today and boast a friendly and surprisingly active user community. There is even a current effort to port Linux to the C64 and C128 machines.

CDE

The **c**ommon **d**esktop **e**nvironment is a popular commercial window manager (and much more -- as its name touts, it is more of a desktop environment) that runs under X-Windows. Free work-alike versions are also available.

chain

Some computer devices support chaining, the ability to string multiple devices in a sequence plugged into just one computer port. Often, but not always, such a chain will require some sort of terminator to mark the end. For an example, a SCSI scanner may be plugged into a SCSI CD-ROM drive that is plugged into a SCSI hard drive that is in turn plugged into the main computer. For all these components to work properly, the scanner would also have to have a proper terminator in use. Device chaining has been around a long time, and it is interesting to note that C64/128 serial devices supported it from the very beginning. Today the most common low-cost chainable devices in use support USB while the fastest low-cost chainable devices in use support FireWire.

character set

Since in reality all a computer can store are series of zeros and ones, representing common things like text takes a little work. The solution is to view the series of zeros and ones instead as a sequence of bytes, and map each one to a particular letter, number, or symbol. The full mapping is called a character set. The most popular character set is commonly referred to as ASCII. The second most popular character set these days is Unicode (and it will probably eventually surpass ASCII). Other fairly common character sets include EBCDIC and PETSCII. They are generally quite different from one another; programs exist to convert between them on most platforms, though. Usually EBCDIC is only found on really old machines.

CISC

Complex **i**nstruction **s**et **c**omputing is one of the two main types of processor design in use today. It is slowly losing popularity to RISC designs; currently all the fastest processors in the world are RISC. The most popular current CISC processor is the x86, but there are also still some 68xx, 65xx, and Z80s in use.

CLI

A command-line interface is a text-based means of communicating with a program, especially an OS. This is the sort of interface used by MS-DOS, or a UNIX shell window.

COBOL

The **C**ommon **B**usiness **O**riented **L**anguage is a language developed back in 1959 and still used by some businesses. While it is relatively portable, it is still disliked by many professional programmers simply because COBOL programs tend to be physically longer than equivalent programs written in almost any other language in common use.

compiled

If a program is compiled, its original human-readable source has been converted into a form more easily used by a computer prior to it being run. Such programs will generally run more quickly than interpreted programs, because time was pre-spent in the compilation phase. A program that compiles other programs is called a compiler.

compression

It is often possible to remove redundant information or capitalize on patterns in data to make a file smaller. Usually when a file has been compressed, it cannot be used until it is uncompressed. Image files are common exceptions, though, as many popular image file formats have compression built-in.

cookie

A cookie is a small file that a web page on another machine writes to your personal machine's disk to store various bits of information. Many people strongly detest cookies and the whole idea of them, and most browsers allow the reception of cookies to be disabled or at least selectively disabled, but it should be noted that both Netscape and MSIE have silent cookie reception enabled by default. Sites that maintain shopping carts or remember a reader's last position have legitimate uses for cookies. Sites without such functionality that still spew cookies with distant (or worse, non-existent) expiration dates should perhaps be treated with a little caution.

CP/M

An early DOS for desktops, CP/M runs on both Z80 and the x86 based machines. CP/M provides only a CLI and there really is not any standard way to get a window manager to run on top of it. It is fairly complex and tricky to use. In spite of all this, CP/M was once the most popular DOS and is still in use today.

crash

If a bug in a program is severe enough, it can cause that program to crash, or to become inoperable without being restarted. On machines that are not multitasking, the entire machine will crash and have to be rebooted. On machines that are only partially multitasking the entire machine will sometimes crash and have to be rebooted. On machines that are fully multitasking, the machine should never crash and require a reboot.

Cray

A Cray is a high-end computer used for research and frequently heavy-duty graphics applications. Modern Crays typically have Solaris for their OS and sport sixty-four RISC processors; older ones had various other configurations. Current top-of-the-line Crays can have over 2000 processors.

crippleware

Crippleware is a variant of shareware that will either self-destruct after its trial period or has built-in limitations to its functionality that get removed after its purchase.

CSS

Cascading style sheets are used in conjunction with HTML and XHTML to define the layout of web pages. While CSS is how current web pages declare how they should be displayed, it tends not to be supported well (if at all) by ancient browsers. XSL performs this same function more generally.

desktop publisher

A program for creating newspapers, magazines, books, etc. Some common desktop publishing programs include FrameMaker, PageMaker, InDesign, and GeoPublish.

DHTML

Dynamic HTML is simply the combined use of both CSS and JavaScript together in the same document; a more extreme form is called AJaX. Note that DHTML is quite different from the similarly named DTML.

dict

A protocol used for looking up definitions across a network (in particular the Internet).

digital camera

A digital camera looks and behaves like a regular camera, except instead of using film, it stores the image it sees in memory as a file for later transfer to a computer. Many digital cameras offer additional storage besides their own internal memory; a few sport some sort of disk but the majority utilize some sort of flash card. Digital cameras currently lack the resolution and color palette of real cameras, but are usually much more convenient for computer applications. Another related device is called a scanner.

DIMM

A physical component used to add RAM to a computer. Similar to, but incompatible with, SIMMs.

DNS

Domain name service is the means by which a name (like www.saugus.net or ftp.saugus.net) gets converted into a real Internet address that points to a particular machine.

DoS

In a denial of service attack, many individual (usually compromised) computers are used to try and simultaneously access the same public resource with the intent of overburdening it so that it will not be able to adequately serve its normal users.

DOS

A disk operating system manages disks and other system resources. Sort of a subset of OSes, sort of an archaic term for the same. MS-DOS is the most popular program currently calling itself a DOS. CP/M was the most popular prior to MS-DOS.

download

To download a file is to copy it from a remote computer to your own. The opposite is upload.

DR-DOS

The DOS currently produced by Caldera (originally produced by Design Research as a successor to CP/M) designed to work like MS-DOS. While similar to CP/M in many ways, it utilizes simpler commands. It provides only a CLI, but either Windows 3.1 or GEOS may be run on top of it to provide a GUI. It only runs on x86 based machines.

driver

A driver is a piece of software that works with the OS to control a particular piece of hardware, like a printer or a scanner or a mouse or whatever.

DRM

Depending upon whom you ask, DRM can stand for either Digital Rights Management or Digital Restrictions Management. In either case, DRM is used to place restrictions upon the usage of digital media ranging from software to music to video.

DTML

The **D**ocument **T**emplate **M**ark-up **L**anguage is a subset of SGML and a superset of HTML used for creating documents that dynamically adapt to external conditions using its own custom tags and a little bit of Python. Note that it is quite different from the similarly named DHTML.

EDBIC

The EDBIC character set is similar to (but less popular than) the ASCII character set in concept, but is significantly different in layout. It tends to be found only on old machines..

emacs

Emacs is both one of the most powerful and one of the most popular text editing programs in existence. Versions can be found for most platforms, and in fact multiple companies make versions, so for a given platform there might even be a choice. There is even a free GNU version available. The drawback with emacs is that it is not in the least bit lightweight. In fact, it goes so far in the other direction that even its advocates will occasionally joke about it. It is however extremely capable. Almost anything that one would need to relating to text can be done with emacs and is probably built-in. Even if one manages to find something that emacs was not built to do, emacs has a built-in Lisp interpreter capable of not only extending its text editing capabilities, but even of being used as a scripting language in its own right.

embedded

An embedded system is a computer that lives inside another device and acts as a component of that device. For example, current cars have an embedded computer under the hood that helps regulate much of their day to day operation.

An embedded file is a file that lives inside another and acts as a portion of that file. This is frequently seen with HTML files having embedded audio files; audio files often embedded in HTML include AU files, MIDI files, SID files, WAV files, AIFF files, and MOD files. Most browsers will ignore these files unless an appropriate plug-in is present.

emulator

An emulator is a program that allows one computer platform to mimic another for the purposes of running its software. Typically (but not always) running a program through an emulator will not be quite as pleasant an experience as running it on the real system.

endian

A processor will be either "big endian" or "little endian" based upon the manner in which it encodes multiple byte values. There is no difference in performance between the two encoding methods, but it is one of the sources of difficulty when reading binary data on different platforms.

environment

An environment (sometimes also called a runtime environment) is a collection of external variable items or parameters that a program can access when run. Information about the computer's hardware and the user can often be found in the environment.

EPOC

EPOC is a lightweight OS. It is most commonly found on the Psion PDA.

extension

Filename extensions originate back in the days of CP/M and basically allow a very rough grouping of different file types by putting a tag at the end of the name. To further complicate matters, the tag is sometimes separated by the name proper by a period "." and sometimes by a tab. While extensions are semi-enforced on CP/M, MS-DOS, and MS-Windows, they have no real meaning aside from convention on other platforms and are only optional.

FAQ

A **f**requently **a**sked **q**uestions file attempts to provide answers for all commonly asked questions related to a given topic.

FireWire

An incredibly fast type of serial port that offers many of the best features of SCSI at a lower price. Faster than most types of parallel port, a single FireWire port is capable of chaining many devices without the need of a terminator. FireWire is similar in many respects to USB but is significantly faster and somewhat more expensive. It is heavily used for connecting audio/video devices to computers, but is also used for connecting storage devices like drives and other assorted devices like printers and scanners.

fixed width

As applied to a font, fixed width means that every character takes up the same amount of space. That is, an "i" will be just as wide as an "m" with empty space being used for padding. The opposite is variable width. The most common fixed width font is Courier.

flash

Flash memory is similar to RAM. It has one significant advantage: it does not lose its contents when power is lost; it has two main disadvantages: it is slower, and it eventually wears out. Flash memory is frequently found in PCMCIA cards.

font

In a simplistic sense, a font can be thought of as the physical description of a character set. While the character set will define what sets of bits map to what letters, numbers, and other symbols, the font will define what each letter, number, and other symbol looks like. Fonts can be either fixed width or variable width and independently, either bitmapped or vectored. The size of the large characters in a font is typically measured in points.

Forth

A language developed in 1970 by Moore. Forth is fairly portable and has versions on many different platforms. While it is no longer an very popular language, many of its ideas and concepts have been carried into other computer programs. In particular, some programs for doing heavy-duty mathematical and engineering work use Forth-like interfaces.

FORTRAN

FORTRAN stands for **for**mula **tran**slation and is the oldest computer language in the world. It is typically compiled and is quite fast. Its primary drawbacks are portability and ease-of-use -- often different FORTRAN compilers on different platforms behave quite differently in spite of standardization efforts in 1966 (FORTRAN 66 or FORTRAN IV), 1978 (FORTRAN 77), and 1991 (FORTRAN 90). Today languages like C and Java are more popular, but FORTRAN is still heavily used in military software. It is somewhat amusing to note that when FORTRAN was first released back in 1958 its advocates thought that it would mean the end of software bugs. In truth of course by making the creation of more complex software practical, computer languages have merely created new types of software bugs.

FreeBSD

A free variant of Berkeley UNIX available for Alpha and x86 based machines. It is not as popular as Linux.

freeware

Freeware is software that is available for free with no strings attached. The quality is often superb as the authors are also generally users.

FTP

The **f**ile **t**ransfer **p**rotocol is one of the most commonly used methods of copying files across the Internet. It has its origins on UNIX machines, but has been adapted to almost every type of computer in existence and is built into many browsers. Most FTP programs have two modes of operation, ASCII, and binary. Transmitting an ASCII file via the ASCII mode of operation is more efficient and cleaner. Transmitting a binary file via the ASCII mode of operation will result in a broken binary file. Thus the FTP programs that do not support both modes of operation will typically only do the binary mode, as binary transfers are capable of transferring both kinds of data without corruption.

gateway

A gateway connects otherwise separate computer networks.

GEOS

The **g**raphic **e**nvironment **o**perating **s**ystem is a lightweight OS with a GUI. It runs on several different processors, including the 65xx (different versions for different machines -- there are versions for the C64, the C128, and the Apple][, each utilizing the relevant custom chip sets), the x86 (although the x86 version is made to run on top of MS-DOS (or PC-DOS or DR-DOS) and is not strictly a full OS or a window manager, rather it is somewhat in between, like Windows 3.1) and numerous different PDAs, embedded devices, and hand-held machines. It was originally designed by Berkeley Softworks (no real relation to the Berkeley of UNIX fame) but is currently in a more interesting state: the company GeoWorks develops and promotes development of GEOS for hand-held devices, PDAs, & and embedded devices and owns (but has ceased further development on) the x86 version. The other versions are owned (and possibly still being developed) by the company CMD.

GHz & **gigahertz**

One gigahertz is equivalent to 1000 megahertz, or 1,000,000,000 hertz.

Glulx

A virtual machine optimized for running interactive fiction, interactive tutorials, and other interactive things of a primarily textual nature. Glulx has been ported to several platforms, and in in many ways an upgrade to the Z-machine.

GNOME

The **GN**U **n**etwork **o**bject **m**odel **e**nvironment is a popular free window manager (and much more -- as its name touts, it is more of a desktop environment) that runs under X-Windows. It is a part of the GNU project.

GNU

GNU stands for **GNU**'s **n**ot **U**NIX and is thus a recursive acronym (and unlike the animal name, the "G" here is pronounced). At any rate, the GNU project is an effort by the Free Software Foundation (FSF) to make all of the traditional UNIX utilities free for whoever wants them. The Free Software Foundation programmers know their stuff, and the quality of the GNU software is on par with the best produced commercially, and often better. All of the GNU software can be downloaded for free or obtained on CD-ROM for a small service fee. Documentation for all GNU software can be downloaded for free or obtained in book form for a small service fee. The Free Software Foundation pays its bills from the collection of service fees and the sale of T-shirts, and exists mostly through volunteer effort. It is based in Cambridge, MA.

gopher

Though not as popular as FTP or http, the gopher protocol is implemented by many browsers and numerous other programs and allows the transfer of files across networks. In some respects it can be thought of as a hybrid between FTP and http, although it tends not to be as good at raw file transfer as FTP and is not as flexible as http. The collection of documents available through gopher is often called "gopherspace", and it should be noted that gopherspace is older than the web. It should also be noted that gopher is not getting as much attention as it once did, and surfing through gopherspace is a little like exploring a ghost town, but there is an interesting VR interface available for it, and some things in gopherspace still have not been copied onto the web.

GUI

A **g**raphical **u**ser **i**nterface is a graphics-based means of communicating with a program, especially an OS or window manager. In fact, a window manager can be thought of as a GUI for a CLI OS.

HP-UX

HP-UX is the version of UNIX designed by Hewlett-Packard to work with their PA-RISC and

68xx based machines.
HTML
The **Hy**pertext **M**ark-up **L**anguage is the language currently most frequently used to express web pages (although it is rapidly being replaced by XHTML). Every browser has the built-in ability to understand HTML. Some browsers can additionally understand Java and browse FTP areas. HTML is a proper subset of SGML.
http
The **h**ypertext **t**ransfer **p**rotocol is the native protocol of browsers and is most typically used to transfer HTML formatted files. The secure version is called "https".
Hurd
The Hurd is the official GNU OS. It is still in development and is not yet supported on too many different processors, but promises to be the most powerful OS available. It (like all the GNU software) is free.
Hz & hertz
Hertz means cycles per second, and makes no assumptions about what is cycling. So, for example, if a fluorescent light flickers once per jiffy, it has a 60 Hz flicker. More typical for computers would be a program that runs once per jiffy and thus has a 60 Hz frequency, or larger units of hertz like kHz, MHz, GHz, or THz.
i18n
Commonly used to abbreviate the word "internationalization". There are eighteen letters between the "i" and the "n". Similar to (and often used along with) i18n.
iCalendar
The iCalendar standard refers to the format used to store calendar type information (including events, to-do items, and journal entries) on the Internet. iCalendar data can be found on some World-Wide-Web pages or attached to e-mail messages.
icon
A small graphical display representing an object, action, or modifier of some sort.
IDE
Loosely speaking, a disk format sometimes used by MS-Windows, Mac OS, AmigaOS, and (rarely) UNIX. EIDE is enhanced IDE; it is much faster. Generally IDE is inferior (but less expensive) to SCSI, but it varies somewhat with system load and the individual IDE and SCSI components themselves. The quick rundown is that: SCSI-I and SCSI-II will almost always outperform IDE; EIDE will almost always outperform SCSI-I and SCSI-II; SCSI-III and UltraSCSI will almost always outperform EIDE; and heavy system loads give an advantage to SCSI. Note that although loosely speaking it is just a format difference, it is deep down a hardware difference.
Inform
A compiled, object-oriented language optimized for creating interactive fiction.
infrared communications
A device with an infrared port can communicate with other devices at a distance by beaming infrared light signals. Two incompatible protocols are used for infrared communications: IrDA and ASK. Many devices support both.
Instant Messenger
AOL's Instant Messenger is is a means of chatting over the Internet in real-time. It allows both open group discussions and private conversations. Instant Messenger uses a different, proprietary protocol from the more standard IRC, and is not supported on as many platforms.
interactive fiction
Interactive fiction (often abbreviated "IF" or "I-F") is a form of literature unique to the computer. While the reader cannot influence the direction of a typical story, the reader plays a more active role in an interactive fiction story and completely controls its direction. Interactive fiction works come in all the sizes and genres available to standard fiction, and in fact are not always even

fiction per se (interactive tutorials exist and are slowly becoming more common).

interpreted

If a program is interpreted, its actual human-readable source is read as it is run by the computer. This is generally a slower process than if the program being run has already been compiled.

intranet

An intranet is a private network. There are many intranets scattered all over the world. Some are connected to the Internet via gateways.

IP

IP is the family of protocols that makes up the Internet. The two most common flavors are TCP/IP and UDP/IP.

IRC

Internet relay chat is a means of chatting over the Internet in real-time. It allows both open group discussions and private conversations. IRC programs are provided by many different companies and will work on many different platforms. AOL's Instant Messenger utilizes a separate incompatible protocol but is otherwise very similar.

IrDA

The Infrared Data Association (IrDA) is a voluntary organization of various manufacturers working together to ensure that the infrared communications between different computers, PDAs, printers, digital cameras, remote controls, etc. are all compatible with each other regardless of brand. The term is also often used to designate an IrDA compliant infrared communications port on a device. Informally, a device able to communicate via IrDA compliant infrared is sometimes simply said to "have IrDA". There is also an earlier, incompatible, and usually slower type of infrared communications still in use called ASK.

IRI

An Internationalized Resource Identifier is just a URI with i18n.

IRIX

The variant of UNIX designed by Silicon Graphics, Inc. IRIX machines are known for their graphics capabilities and were initially optimized for multimedia applications.

ISDN

An integrated service digital network line can be simply looked at as a digital phone line. ISDN connections to the Internet can be four times faster than the fastest regular phone connection, and because it is a digital connection a modem is not needed. Any computer hooked up to ISDN will typically require other special equipment in lieu of the modem, however. Also, both phone companies and ISPs charge more for ISDN connections than regular modem connections.

ISP

An Internet service provider is a company that provides Internet support for other entities. AOL (America Online) is a well-known ISP.

Java

A computer language designed to be both fairly lightweight and extremely portable. It is tightly bound to the web as it is the primary language for web applets. There has also been an OS based on Java for use on small hand-held, embedded, and network computers. It is called JavaOS. Java can be either interpreted or compiled. For web applet use it is almost always interpreted. While its interpreted form tends not to be very fast, its compiled form can often rival languages like C++ for speed. It is important to note however that speed is not Java's primary purpose -- raw speed is considered secondary to portabilty and ease of use.

JavaScript

JavaScript (in spite of its name) has nothing whatsoever to do with Java (in fact, it's arguably more like Newton Script than Java). JavaScript is an interpreted language built into a browser to provide a relatively simple means of adding interactivity to web pages. It is only supported on a few different browsers, and tends not to work exactly the same on different versions. Thus its use on the Internet is somewhat restricted to fairly simple programs. On intranets where there are usually fewer browser versions in use, JavaScript has been used to implement much more complex and impressive programs.

jiffy

A jiffy is 1/60 of a second. Jiffies are to seconds as seconds are to minutes.

joystick

A joystick is a physical device typically used to control objects on a computer screen. It is frequently used for games and sometimes used in place of a mouse.

JSON

The JSON is used for data interchange between programs, an area in which the ubiquitous XML is not too well-suited. JSON is lightweight and works extremely cleanly with languages languages including JavaScript, Python, Java, C++, and many others.

JSON-RPC

JSON-RPC is like XML-RPC but is significantly more lightweight since it uses JSON in lieu of XML.

KDE

The **K** desktop environment is a popular free window manager (and much more -- as its name touts, it is more of a desktop environment) that runs under X-Windows.

Kerberos

Kerberos is a network authentication protocol. Basically it preserves the integrity of passwords in any untrusted network (like the Internet). Kerberized applications work hand-in-hand with sites that support Kerberos to ensure that passwords cannot be stolen.

kernel

The very heart of an OS is often called its kernel. It will usually (at minimum) provide some libraries that give programmers access to its various features.

kHz & **kilohertz**

One kilohertz is equivalent to 1000 hertz. Some older computers have clock speeds measured in kHz.

l10n

Commonly used to abbreviate the word "localization". There are ten letters between the "l" and the "n". Similar to (and often used along with) i18n.

LDAP

The **L**ightweight **D**irectory **A**ccess **P**rotocol provides a means of sharing address book type of information across an intranet or even across the Internet. Note too that "address book type of information" here is pretty broad; it often includes not just human addresses, but machine addresses, printer configurations, and similar.

library

A selection of routines used by programmers to make computers do particular things.

lightweight

Something that is lightweight will not consume computer resources (such as RAM and disk space) too much and will thus run on less expensive computer systems.

Linux

Believe it or not, one of the fastest, most robust, and powerful multitasking OSes is available for free. Linux can be downloaded for free or be purchased on CD-ROM for a small service charge. A handful of companies distribute Linux including Red Hat, Debian, Caldera, and many others. Linux is also possibly available for more hardware combinations than any other OS (with the possible exception of NetBSD. Supported processors include: Alpha, PowerPC, SPARC, x86, and 68xx. Most processors currently not supported are currently works-in-progress or even available in beta. For example, work is currently underway to provide support for PA-RISC, 65xx, StrongARM, and Z80. People have even successfully gotten Linux working on PDAs. As you may have guessed, Linux can be made quite lightweight. Linux is a variant of UNIX and as such, most of the traditional UNIX software will run on Linux. This especially includes the GNU software, most of which comes with the majority of Linux distributions. Fast, reliable, stable, and inexpensive, Linux is popular with ISPs, software developers, and home hobbyists alike.

Lisp

Lisp stands for **lis**t processing and is the second oldest computer language in the world. Being developed in 1959, it lost the title to FORTRAN by only a few months. It is typically interpreted, but compilers are available for some platforms. Attempts were made to standardize the language, and the standard version is called "Common Lisp". There have also been efforts to simplify the language, and the results of these efforts is another language called Scheme. Lisp is a fairly portable language, but is not particularly fast. Today, Lisp is most widely used with AI software.

load

There are two popular meanings for load. The first means to fetch some data or a program from a disk and store it in memory. The second indicates the amount of work a component (especially a processor) is being made to do.

Logo

Logo is an interpreted language designed by Papert in 1966 to be a tool for helping people (especially kids) learn computer programming concepts. In addition to being used for that purpose, it is often used as a language for controlling mechanical robots and other similar devices. Logo interfaces even exist for building block / toy robot sets. Logo uses a special graphics cursor called "the turtle", and Logo is itself sometimes called "Turtle Graphics". Logo is quite portable but not particularly fast. Versions can be found on almost every computer platform in the world. Additionally, some other languages (notably some Pascal versions) provide Logo-like interfaces for graphics-intensive programming.

lossy

If a process is lossy, it means that a little quality is lost when it is performed. If a format is lossy, it means that putting data into that format (or possibly even manipulating it in that format) will cause some slight loss. Lossy processes and formats are typically used for performance or resource utilization reasons. The opposite of lossy is lossless.

Lua

Lua is a simple interpreted language. It is extremely portable, and free versions exist for most platforms.

Mac OS

Mac OS is the OS used on Macintosh computers. There are two distinctively different versions of it; everything prior to version 10 (sometimes called Mac OS Classic) and everything version 10 or later (called Mac OS X).

Mac OS Classic

The OS created by Apple and originally used by Macs is frequently (albeit slightly incorrectly) referred to as Mac OS Classic (officially Mac OS Classic is this original OS running under the modern Mac OS X in emulation. Mac OS combines the functionality of both an OS and a window manager and is often considered to be the easiest OS to use. It is partially multitasking but will still sometimes crash when dealing with a buggy program. It is probably the second most popular OS, next only to Windows 'XP (although it is quickly losing ground to Mac OS X) and has excellent driver support and boasts a fair selection of games. Mac OS will run on PowerPC and 68xx based machines.

Mac OS X

Mac OS X (originally called Rhapsody) is the industrial strength OS produced by Apple to run on both PowerPC and x86 systems (replacing what is often referred to as Mac OS Classic. Mac OS X is at its heart a variant of UNIX and possesses its underlying power (and the ability to run many of the traditional UNIX tools, including the GNU tools). It also was designed to mimic other OSes on demand via what it originally refered to as "boxes" (actually high-performance emulators); it has the built-in capability to run programs written for older Mac OS (via its "BlueBox", officially called Mac OS Classic) and work was started on making it also run Windows '95 / '98 / ME software (via what was called its "YellowBox"). There are also a few rumors going around that future versions may even be able to run Newton software (via the "GreenBox"). It provides a selection of two window managers built-in: Aqua and X-Windows (with Aqua being the default).

machine language

Machine language consists of the raw numbers that can be directly understood by a particular processor. Each processor's machine language will be different from other processors' machine language. Although called "machine language", it is not usually what people think of when talking about computer languages. Machine language dressed up with mnemonics to make it a bit more human-readable is called assembly language.

Macintosh

A Macintosh (or a Mac for short) is a computer system that has Mac OS for its OS. There are a few different companies that have produced Macs, but by far the largest is Apple. The oldest Macs are based on the 68xx processor; somewhat more recent Macs on the PowerPC processor, and current Macs on the x86 processor. The Macintosh was really the first general purpose computer to employ a GUI.

MacTel

An x86 based system running some flavor of Mac OS.

mainframe

A mainframe is any computer larger than a small piece of furniture. A modern mainframe is more powerful than a modern workstation, but more expensive and more difficult to maintain.

MathML

The **Math M**ark-up **L**anguage is a subset of XML used to represent mathematical formulae and equations. Typically it is found embedded within XHTML documents, although as of this writing not all popular browsers support it.

megahertz

A million cycles per second, abbreviated MHz. This is often used misleadingly to indicate processor speed, because while one might expect that a higher number would indicate a faster processor, that logic only holds true within a given type of processors as different types of processors are capable of doing different amounts of work within a cycle. For a current example, either a 200 MHz PowerPC or a 270 MHz SPARC will outperform a 300 MHz Pentium.

Merced

The Merced is a RISC processor developed by Intel with help from Hewlett-Packard and possibly Sun. It is just starting to be released, but is intended to eventually replace both the x86 and PA-RISC processors. Curiously, HP is recommending that everyone hold off using the first release and instead wait for the second one. It is expected some day to be roughly as fast as an Alpha or PowerPC. It is expected to be supported by future versions of Solaris, Windows-NT, HP-UX, Mac OS X, and Linux. The current semi-available Merced processor is called the Itanium. Its overall schedule is way behind, and some analysts predict that it never will really be released in significant quanitities.

MFM

Loosely speaking, An old disk format sometimes used by CP/M, MS-DOS, and MS-Windows. No longer too common as it cannot deliver close to the performance of either SCSI or IDE.

middleware

Software designed to sit in between an OS and applications. Common examples are Java and Tcl/Tk.

MIME

The **m**ulti-purpose **I**nternet **m**ail **e**xtensions specification describes a means of sending non-

ASCII data (such as images, sounds, foreign symbols, etc.) through e-mail. It commonly utilizes bcode.

MMX

Multimedia extensions were built into some x86 CPUs to provide better performance for certain operations, most notably graphics and sound. It is similar to AltiVec on the PowerPC CPUs. Like AltiVec, it requires special software for full performance benefits to be realized.

MOB

A **mo**vable **ob**ject is a graphical object that is manipulated separately from the background. These are seen all the time in computer games. When implemented in hardware, MOBs are sometimes called sprites.

Modula-2 & Modula-3

Modula-2 is a procedural language based on Pascal by its original author in around the 1977 - 1979 time period. Modula-3 is an intended successor that adds support for object-oriented constructs (among other things). Modula-2 can be either compiled or interpreted, while Modula-3 tends to be just a compiled language.

MOTD

A **m**essage **o**f **t**he **d**ay. Many computers (particularly more capable ones) are configured to display a MOTD when accessed remotely.

Motif

Motif is a popular commercial window manager that runs under X-Windows. Free work-alike versions are also available.

MS-DOS

The DOS produced by Microsoft. Early versions of it bear striking similarities to the earlier CP/M, but it utilizes simpler commands. It provides only a CLI, but either OS/2, Windows 3.1, Windows '95, Windows '98, Windows ME, or GEOS may be run on top of it to provide a GUI. It only runs on x86 based machines.

MS-Windows

MS-Windows is the name collectively given to several somewhat incompatible OSes all produced by Microsoft. They are: Windows CE, Windows NT, Windows 3.1, Windows '95, Windows '98, Windows ME, Windows 2000, and Windows XP.

MUD

A **m**ulti-**u**ser **d**imension (also sometimes called multi-user dungeon, but in either case abbreviated to "MUD") is sort of a combination between the online chatting abilities provided by something like IRC and a role-playing game. A MUD built with object oriented principles in mind is called a "Multi-user dimension object-oriented", or MOO. Yet another variant is called a "multi-user shell", or MUSH. Still other variants are called multi-user role-playing environments (MURPE) and multi-user environments (MUSE). There are probably more. In all cases the differences will be mostly academic to the regular user, as the same software is used to connect to all of them. Software to connect to MUDs can be found for most platforms, and there are even Java based ones that can run from within a browser.

multitasking

Some OSes have built into them the ability to do several things at once. This is called multitasking, and has been in use since the late sixties / early seventies. Since this ability is built into the software, the overall system will be slower running two things at once than it will be running just one thing. A system may have more than one processor built into it though, and such a system will be capable of running multiple things at once with less of a performance hit.

nagware

Nagware is a variant of shareware that will frequently remind its users to register.

NetBSD

A free variant of Berkeley UNIX available for Alpha, x86, 68xx, PA-RISC, SPARC, PowerPC, ARM, and many other types of machines. Its emphasis is on portability.

netiquette

The established conventions of online politeness are called netiquette. Some conventions vary from site to site or online medium to online medium; others are pretty standard everywhere. Newbies are often unfamiliar with the conventional rules of netiquette and sometimes embarrass themselves accordingly. Be sure not to send that incredibly important e-mail message before reading about netiquette.

newbie

A newbie is a novice to the online world or computers in general.

news

Usenet news can generally be thought of as public e-mail as that is generally the way it behaves. In reality, it is implemented by different software and is often accessed by different programs. Different newsgroups adhere to different topics, and some are "moderated", meaning that humans will try to manually remove off-topic posts, especially spam. Most established newsgroups have a FAQ, and people are strongly encouraged to read the FAQ prior to posting.

Newton

Although Newton is officially the name of the lightweight OS developed by Apple to run on its MessagePad line of PDAs, it is often used to mean the MessagePads (and compatible PDAs) themselves and thus the term "Newton OS" is often used for clarity. The Newton OS is remarkably powerful; it is fully multitasking in spite of the fact that it was designed for small machines. It is optimized for hand-held use, but will readily transfer data to all manner of desktop machines. Historically it was the first PDA. Recently Apple announced that it will discontinue further development of the Newton platform, but will instead work to base future hand-held devices on either Mac OS or Mac OS X with some effort dedicated to making the new devices capable of running current Newton programs.

Newton book

Newton books provide all the functionality of ordinary books but add searching and hypertext capabilities. The format was invented for the Newton to provide a means of making volumes of data portable, and is particularly popular in the medical community as most medical references are available as Newton books and carrying around a one pound Newton is preferable to carrying around twenty pounds of books, especially when it comes to looking up something. In addition to medical books, numerous references, most of the classics, and many contemporary works of fiction are available as Newton books. Most fiction is available for free, most references cost money. Newton books are somewhat more capable than the similar Palm DOC; both are specific types of e-books.

Newton Script

A intepreted, object-oriented language for Newton MessagePad computers.

nybble

A nybble is half a byte, or four bits. It is a case of computer whimsy; it only stands to reason that a small byte should be called a nybble. Some authors spell it with an "i" instead of the "y", but the "y" is the original form.

object-oriented

While the specifics are well beyond the scope of this document, the term "object-oriented" applies to a philosophy of software creation. Often this philosophy is referred to as object-oriented design (sometimes abbreviated as OOD), and programs written with it in mind are referred to as object-oriented programs (often abbreviated OOP). Programming languages designed to help facilitate it are called object-oriented languages (sometimes abbreviated as OOL) and databases built with it in mind are called object-oriented databases (sometimes abbreviated as OODB or less fortunately OOD). The general notion is that an object-oriented approach to creating software starts with modeling the real-world problems trying to be solved in familiar real-world ways, and carries the analogy all the way down to structure of the program. This is of course a great over-simplification. Numerous object-oriented programming languages exist including: Java, C++, Modula-2, Newton Script, and ADA.

Objective-C & ObjC

Objective-C (often called "ObjC" for short) is a compiled object-oriented language. Based heavily on C, Objective-C is nearly as fast and can often be thought of as being just C with added features. Note that it was developed independently of C++; its object-oriented extensions are more in the style of Smalltalk. It is however related to Objective-C++.

Objective-C++ & ObjC++

Objective-C++ (often called "ObjC++" for short) is a curious hybrid of Objective-C and C++, allowing the syntax of both to coexist in the same source files.

office suite

An office suite is a collection of programs including at minimum a word processor, spreadsheet, drawing program, and minimal database program. Some common office suites include MS-Office, AppleWorks, ClarisWorks, GeoWorks, Applixware, Corel Office, and StarOffice.

open source

Open source software goes one step beyond freeware. Not only does it provide the software for free, it provides the original source code used to create the software. Thus, curious users can poke around with it to see how it works, and advanced users can modify it to make it work better for them. By its nature, open souce software is pretty well immune to all types of computer virus.

OpenBSD

A free variant of Berkeley UNIX available for Alpha, x86, 68xx, PA-RISC, SPARC, and PowerPC based machines. Its emphasis is on security.

OpenDocument & ODF

OpenDocument (or ODF for short) is the suite of open, XML-based office suite application formats defined by the OASIS consortium. It defines a platform-neutral, non-proprietary way of storing documents.

OpenGL

A low-level 3D graphics library with an emphasis on speed developed by SGI.

OS/2

OS/2 is the OS designed by IBM to run on x86 based machines. It is semi-compatible with MS-Windows. IBM's more industrial strength OS is called AIX.

PA-RISC

The PA-RISC is a RISC processor developed by Hewlett-Packard. It is currently produced only by HP. At the moment only one OS runs on PA-RISC based machines: HP-UX. There is an effort underway to port Linux to them, though.

Palm DOC

Palm DOC files are quite similar to (but slightly less capable than) Newton books. They were designed for Palm Pilots but can now be read on a couple other platforms, too. They are a specific type of e-book.

Palm Pilot

The Palm Pilot (also called both just Palm and just Pilot, officially now just Palm) is the most popular PDA currently in use. It is one of the least capable PDAs, but it is also one of the smallest and least expensive. While not as full featured as many of the other PDAs (such as the Newton) it performs what features it does have quite well and still remains truly pocket-sized.

parallel

Loosely speaking, parallel implies a situation where multiple things can be done simultaneously, like having multiple check-out lines each serving people all at once. Parallel connections are by their nature more expensive than serial ones, but usually faster. Also, in a related use of the word, often multitasking computers are said to be capable of running multiple programs in parallel.

partition

Sometimes due to hardware limitations, disks have to be divided into smaller pieces. These pieces are called partitions.

Pascal

Named after the mathematician Blaise Pascal, Pascal is a language designed by Niklaus Wirth originally in 1968 (and heavily revised in 1972) mostly for purposes of education and training people how to write computer programs. It is a typically compiled language but is still usually slower than C or FORTRAN. Wirth also created a more powerful object-oriented Pascal-like language called Modula-2.

PC-DOS

The DOS produced by IBM designed to work like MS-DOS. Early versions of it bear striking similarities to the earlier CP/M, but it utilizes simpler commands. It provides only a CLI, but either Windows 3.1 or GEOS may be run on top of it to provide a GUI. It only runs on x86 based machines.

PCMCIA

The **P**ersonal **C**omputer **M**emory **C**ard **I**nternational **A**ssociation is a standards body that concern themselves with PC Card technology. Often the PC Cards themselves are referred to as "PCMCIA cards". Frequently flash memory can be found in PC card form.

Perl

Perl is an interpreted language extremely popular for web applications.

PET

The Commodore PET (**P**ersonal **E**lectronic **T**ransactor) is an early (circa 1977-1980, around the same time as the Apple][) home computer featuring a ROM-based BASIC developed by Microsoft which it uses as a default "OS". It is based on the 65xx family of processors and is the precursor to the VIC-20.

PETSCII

The PETSCII character set gets its name from "**PET ASCII**; it is a variant of the ASCII character set originally developed for the Commodore PET that swaps the upper and lower case characters and adds over a hundred graphic characters in addition to other small changes. If you encounter some text that seems to have uppercase where lowercase is expected and vice-versa, it is probably a PETSCII file.

PHP

Named with a recursive acronym (PHP: Hypertext Preprocessor), PHP provides a means of creating web pages that dynamically modify themselves on the fly.

ping

Ping is a protocol designed to check across a network to see if a particular computer is "alive" or not. Computers that recognize the ping will report back their status. Computers that are down will not report back anything at all.

pixel

The smallest distinct point on a computer display is called a pixel.

plug-in

A plug-in is a piece of software designed not to run on its own but rather work in cooperation with a separate application to increase that application's abilities.

point

There are two common meanings for this word. The first is in the geometric sense; a position in space without size. Of course as applied to computers it must take up some space in practise (even if not in theory) and it is thus sometimes synonomous with pixel. The other meaning is related most typically to fonts and regards size. The exact meaning of it in this sense will unfortunately vary somewhat from person to person, but will often mean 1/72 of an inch. Even when it does not exactly mean 1/72 of an inch, larger point sizes always indicate larger fonts.

PowerPC

The PowerPC is a RISC processor developed in a collaborative effort between IBM, Apple, and Motorola. It is currently produced by a few different companies, of course including its original developers. A few different OSes run on PowerPC based machines, including Mac OS, AIX, Solaris, Windows NT, Linux, Mac OS X, BeOS, and AmigaOS. At any given time, the fastest processor in the world is usually either a PowerPC or an Alpha, but sometimes SPARCs and PA-RISCs make the list, too.

proprietary
This simply means to be supplied by only one vendor. It is commonly misused. Currently, most processors are non-proprietary, some systems are non-proprietary, and every OS (except for arguably Linux) is proprietary.

protocol
A protocol is a means of communication used between computers. As long as both computers recognize the same protocol, they can communicate without too much difficulty over the same network or even via a simple direct modem connection regardless whether or not they are themselves of the same type. This means that WinTel boxes, Macs, Amigas, UNIX machines, etc., can all talk with one another provided they agree on a common protocol first.

Psion
The Psion is a fairly popular brand of PDA. Generally, it is in between a Palm and a Newton in capability. It runs the EPOC OS.

Python
Python is an interpreted, object-oriented language popular for Internet applications. It is extremely portable with free versions existing for virtually every platform.

queue
A queue is a waiting list of things to be processed. Many computers provide printing queues, for example. If something is being printed and the user requests that another item be printed, the second item will sit in the printer queue until the first item finishes printing at which point it will be removed from the queue and get printed itself.

QuickDraw
A high-level 3D graphics library with an emphasis on quick development time created by Apple.

RAM
Random access memory is the short-term memory of a computer. Any information stored in RAM will be lost if power goes out, but the computer can read from RAM far more quickly than from a drive.

random access
Also called "dynamic access" this indicates that data can be selected without having to skip over earlier data first. This is the way that a CD, record, laserdisc, or DVD will behave -- it is easy to selectively play a particular track without having to fast forward through earlier tracks. The other common behavior is called sequential access.

RDF
The Resource Description Framework is built upon an XML base and provides a more modern means of accessing data from Internet resources. It can provide metadata (including annotations) for web pages making (among other things) searching more capable. It is also being used to refashion some existing formats like RSS and iCalendar; in the former case it is already in place (at least for newer RSS versions), but it is still experimental in the latter case.

real-time
Something that happens in real-time will keep up with the events around it and never give any sort of "please wait" message.

Rexx
The Restructured Extended Executor is an interpreted language designed primarily to be embedded in other applications in order to make them consistently programmable, but also to be easy to learn and understand.

RISC
Reduced instruction set computing is one of the two main types of processor design in use

today, the other being CISC. The fastest processors in the world today are all RISC designs. There are several popular RISC processors, including Alphas, ARMs, PA-RISCs, PowerPCs, and SPARCs.

robot

A robot (or 'bot for short) in the computer sense is a program designed to automate some task, often just sending messages or collecting information. A spider is a type of robot designed to traverse the web performing some task (usually collecting data).

robust

The adjective robust is used to describe programs that are better designed, have fewer bugs, and are less likely to crash.

ROM

Read-only memory is similar to RAM only cannot be altered and does not lose its contents when power is removed.

RSS

RSS stands for either Rich Site Summary, Really Simple Syndication, or RDF Site Summary, depending upon whom you ask. The general idea is that it can provide brief summaries of articles that appear in full on a web site. It is well-formed XML, and newer versions are even more specifically well-formed RDF.

Ruby

Ruby is an interpreted, object-oriented language. Ruby was fairly heavily influenced by Perl, so people familiar with that language can typically transition to Ruby easily.

scanner

A scanner is a piece of hardware that will examine a picture and produce a computer file that represents what it sees. A digital camera is a related device. Each has its own limitations.

Scheme

Scheme is a typically interpreted computer language. It was created in 1975 in an attempt to make Lisp simpler and more consistent. Scheme is a fairly portable language, but is not particularly fast.

script

A script is a series of OS commands. The term "batch file" means much the same thing, but is a bit dated. Typically the same sort of situations in which one would say DOS instead of OS, it would also be appropriate to say batch file instead of script. Scripts can be run like programs, but tend to perform simpler tasks. When a script is run, it is always interpreted.

SCSI

Loosely speaking, a disk format sometimes used by MS-Windows, Mac OS, AmigaOS, and (almost always) UNIX. Generally SCSI is superior (but more expensive) to IDE, but it varies somewhat with system load and the individual SCSI and IDE components themselves. The quick rundown is that: SCSI-I and SCSI-II will almost always outperform IDE; EIDE will almost always outperform SCSI-I and SCSI-II; SCSI-III and UltraSCSI will almost always outperform EIDE; and heavy system loads give an advantage to SCSI. Note that although loosely speaking it is just a format difference, it is deep down a hardware difference.

sequential access

This indicates that data cannot be selected without having to skip over earlier data first. This is the way that a cassette or video tape will behave. The other common behavior is called random access.

serial

Loosely speaking, serial implies something that has to be done linearly, one at a time, like people being served in a single check-out line. Serial connections are by their nature less expensive than parallel connections (including things like SCSI) but are typically slower.

server

A server is a computer designed to provide various services for an entire network. It is typically either a workstation or a mainframe because it will usually be expected to handle far greater loads than ordinary desktop systems. The load placed on servers also necessitates that they utilize robust OSes, as a crash on a system that is currently being used by many people is far worse than a crash on a system that is only being used by one person.

SGML
The **S**tandard **G**eneralized **M**ark-up **L**anguage provides an extremely generalized level of mark-up. More common mark-up languages like HTML and XML are actually just popular subsets of SGML.

shareware
Shareware is software made for profit that allows a trial period before purchase. Typically shareware can be freely downloaded, used for a period of weeks (or sometimes even months), and either purchased or discarded after it has been learned whether or not it will satisfy the user's needs.

shell
A CLI designed to simplify complex OS commands. Some OSes (like AmigaOS, the Hurd, and UNIX) have built-in support to make the concurrent use of multiple shells easy. Common shells include the Korn Shell (ksh), the Bourne Shell (sh or bsh), the Bourne-Again Shell, (bash or bsh), the C-Shell (csh), etc.

SIMM
A physical component used to add RAM to a computer. Similar to, but incompatible with, DIMMs.

Smalltalk
Smalltalk is an efficient language for writing computer programs. Historically it is one of the first object-oriented languages, and is not only used today in its pure form but shows its influence in other languages like Objective-C.

Solaris
Solaris is the commercial variant of UNIX currently produced by Sun. It is an industrial strength, nigh bulletproof, powerful multitasking OS that will run on SPARC, x86, and PowerPC based machines.

spam
Generally spam is unwanted, unrequested e-mail or Usenet news. It is typically sent out in bulk to huge address lists that were automatically generated by various robots endlessly searching the Internet and newsgroups for things that resemble e-mail addresses. The legality of spam is a topic of much debate; it is at best only borderline legal, and spammers have been successfully persecuted in some states.

SPARC
The SPARC is a RISC processor developed by Sun. The design was more or less released to the world, and it is currently produced by around a dozen different companies too numerous to even bother mentioning. It is worth noting that even computers made by Sun typically sport SPARCs made by other companies. A couple different OSes run on SPARC based machines, including Solaris, SunOS, and Linux. Some of the newer SPARC models are called UltraSPARCs.

sprite
The term sprite originally referred to a small MOB, usually implemented in hardware. Lately it is also being used to refer to a single image used piecemeal within a Web site in order to avoid incurring the time penalty of downloading multiple files.

SQL
SQL (pronounced **Sequel**) is an interpreted language specially designed for database access. It is supported by virtually every major modern database system.

Sugar
The window manager used by the OLPC XO. It is made to run on top of Linux.

SunOS

SunOS is the commercial variant of UNIX formerly produced (but still supported) by Sun.

SVG

Scalable **V**ector **G**raphics data is an XML file that is used to hold graphical data that can be resized without loss of quality. SVG data can be kept in its own file, or even embedded within a web page (although not all browsers are capable of displaying such data).

Tcl/Tk

The **T**ool **C**ommand **L**anguage is a portable interpreted computer language designed to be easy to use. Tk is a GUI toolkit for Tcl. Tcl is a fairly popular language for both integrating existing applications and for creating Web applets (note that applets written in Tcl are often called Tcklets). Tcl/Tk is available for free for most platforms, and plug-ins are available to enable many browsers to play Tcklets.

TCP/IP

TCP/IP is a protocol for computer networks. The Internet is largely built on top of TCP/IP (it is the more reliable of the two primary Internet Protocols -- TCP stands for **T**ransmission **C**ontrol **P**rotocol).

terminator

A terminator is a dedicated device used to mark the end of a device chain (as is most typically found with SCSI devices). If such a chain is not properly terminated, weird results can occur.

TEX

TEX (pronounced "tek") is a freely available, industrial strength typesetting program that can be run on many different platforms. These qualities make it exceptionally popular in schools, and frequently software developed at a university will have its documentation in TEX format. TEX is not limited to educational use, though; many professional books were typeset with TEX. TEX's primary drawback is that it can be quite difficult to set up initially.

THz & terahertz

One terahertz is equivalent to 1000 gigahertz.

TrackBack

TrackBacks essentially provide a means whereby different web sites can post messages to one another not just to inform each other about citations, but also to alert one another of related resources. Typically, a blog may display quotations from another blog through the use of TrackBacks.

UDP/IP

UDP/IP is a protocol for computer networks. It is the faster of the two primary Internet **P**rotocols. UDP stands for **U**ser **D**atagram Protocol.

Unicode

The Unicode character set is a superset of the ASCII character set with provisions made for handling international symbols and characters from other languages. Unicode is sixteen bit, so takes up roughly twice the space as simple ASCII, but is correspondingly more flexible.

UNIX

UNIX is a family of OSes, each being made by a different company or organization but all offering a very similar look and feel. It can not quite be considered non-proprietary, however, as the differences between different vendor's versions can be significant (it is still generally possible to switch from one vendor's UNIX to another without too much effort; today the differences between different UNIXes are similar to the differences between the different MS-Windows; historically there were two different UNIX camps, Berkeley / BSD and AT&T / System V, but the assorted vendors have worked together to minimalize the differences). The free variant Linux is one of the closest things to a current, non-proprietary OS; its development is controlled by a non-profit organization and its distribution is provided by several companies. UNIX is powerful; it is fully multitasking and can do pretty much anything that any OS can do (look to the Hurd if you need a more powerful OS). With power comes complexity, however, and

UNIX tends not to be overly friendly to beginners (although those who think UNIX is difficult or cryptic apparently have not used CP/M). Window managers are available for UNIX (running under X-Windows) and once properly configured common operations will be almost as simple on a UNIX machine as on a Mac. Out of all the OSes in current use, UNIX has the greatest range of hardware support. It will run on machines built around many different processors. Lightweight versions of UNIX have been made to run on PDAs, and in the other direction, full featured versions make full advantage of all the resources on large, multi-processor machines. Some different UNIX versions include Solaris, Linux, IRIX, AIX, SunOS, FreeBSD, Digital UNIX, HP-UX, NetBSD, OpenBSD, etc.

upload

To upload a file is to copy it from your computer to a remote computer. The opposite is download.

UPS

An **u**ninterrupted **p**ower **s**upply uses heavy duty batteries to help smooth out its input power source.

URI

A **U**niform **R**esource **I**dentifier is basically just a unique address for almost any type of resource. It is similar to but more general than a URL; in fact, it may also be a URN.

URL

A **U**niform **R**esource **L**ocator is basically just an address for a file that can be given to a browser. It starts with a protocol type (such as http, ftp, or gopher) and is followed by a colon, machine name, and file name in UNIX style. Optionally an octothorpe character "#" and and arguments will follow the file name; this can be used to further define position within a page and perform a few other tricks. Similar to but less general than a URI.

URN

A **U**niform **R**esource **N**ame is basically just a unique address for almost any type of resource unlike a URL it will probably not resolve with a browser.

USB

A really fast type of serial port that offers many of the best features of SCSI without the price. Faster than many types of parallel port, a single USB port is capable of chaining many devices without the need of a terminator. USB is much slower (but somewhat less expensive) than FireWire.

uucode

The point of uucode is to allow 8-bit binary data to be transferred through the more common 7-bit ASCII channels (most especially e-mail). The facilities for dealing with uucoded files exist for many different machine types, and the most common programs are called "uuencode" for encoding the original binary file into a 7-bit file and "uudecode" for restoring the original binary file from the encoded one. Sometimes different uuencode and uudecode programs will work in subtly different manners causing annoying compatibility problems. Bcode was invented to provide the same service as uucode but to maintain a tighter standard.

variable width

As applied to a font, variable width means that different characters will have different widths as appropriate. For example, an "i" will take up much less space than an "m". The opposite of variable width is fixed width. The terms "proportional width" and "proportionally spaced" mean the same thing as variable width. Some common variable width fonts include Times, Helvetica, and Bookman.

VAX

The VAX is a computer platform developed by Digital. Its plural is VAXen. VAXen are large expensive machines that were once quite popular in large businesses; today modern UNIX workstations have all the capability of VAXen but take up much less space. Their OS is called VMS.

vector

This term has two common meanings. The first is in the geometric sense: a vector defines a direction and magnitude. The second concerns the formatting of fonts and images. If a font is a vector font or an image is a vector image, it is defined as lines of relative size and direction rather than as collections of pixels (the method used in bitmapped fonts and images). This makes it easier to change the size of the font or image, but puts a bigger load on the device that has to display the font or image. The term "outline font" means the same thing as vector font.

Veronica & Veronica2

Although traditionally written as a proper name, Veronica is actually an acronym for "**v**ery **e**asy **r**odent-**o**riented **n**etwide **i**ndex to **c**omputerized **a**rchives", where the "rodent" refers to gopher. The acronym was obviously a little forced to go along with the pre-existing (and now largely unused) Archie, in order to have a little fun with a comic book reference. Regardless, Veronica (or these days more likely Veronica2) is essentially a search engine for gopher resources.

VIC-20

The Commodore VIC-20 computer sold millions of units and is generally considered to have been the first affordable home computer. It features a ROM-based BASIC and uses it as a default "OS". It is based on the 65xx family of processors. VIC (in case you are wondering) can stand for either **v**ideo **i**nterface **c** or **v**ideo **i**nterface **c**omputer. The VIC-20 is the precursor to the C64/128.

virtual machine

A virtual machine is a machine completely defined and implemented in software rather than hardware. It is often referred to as a "runtime environment"; code compiled for such a machine is typically called bytecode.

virtual memory

This is a scheme by which disk space is made to substitute for the more expensive RAM space. Using it will often enable a comptuer to do things it could not do without it, but it will also often result in an overall slowing down of the system. The concept of swap space is very similar.

virtual reality

Virtual reality (often called VR for short) is generally speaking an attempt to provide more natural, human interfaces to software. It can be as simple as a pseudo 3D interface or as elaborate as an isolated room in which the computer can control the user's senses of vision, hearing, and even smell and touch.

virus

A virus is a program that will seek to duplicate itself in memory and on disks, but in a subtle way that will not immediately be noticed. A computer on the same network as an infected computer or that uses an infected disk (even a floppy) or that downloads and runs an infected program can itself become infected. A virus can only spread to computers of the same platform. For example, on a network consisting of a WinTel box, a Mac, and a Linux box, if one machine acquires a virus the other two will probably still be safe. Note also that different platforms have different general levels of resistance; UNIX machines are almost immune, Win '95 / '98 / ME / XP is quite vulnerable, and most others lie somewhere in between.

VMS

The industrial strength OS that runs on VAXen.

VoIP

VoIP means "Voice over IP" and it is quite simply a way of utilizing the Internet (or even in some cases intranets) for telephone conversations. The primary motivations for doing so are cost and convenience as VoIP is significantly less expensive than typical telephone long distance packages, plus one high speed Internet connection can serve for multiple phone lines.

VRML

A **V**irtual **R**eality **M**odeling **L**anguage file is used to represent VR objects. It has essentially been superceded by X3D.

W3C

The World Wide Web Consortium (usually abbreviated W3C) is a non-profit, advisory body that makes suggestions on the future direction of the World Wide Web, HTML, CSS, and browsers.

Waba

An extremely lightweight subset of Java optimized for use on PDAs.

WebDAV

WebDAV stands for Web-based Distributed Authoring and Versioning, and is designed to provide a way of editing Web-based resources in place. It serves as a more modern (and often more secure) replacement for FTP in many cases.

WebTV

A WebTV box hooks up to an ordinary television set and displays web pages. It will not display them as well as a dedicated computer.

window manager

A window manager is a program that acts as a graphical go-between for a user and an OS. It provides a GUI for the OS. Some OSes incorporate the window manager into their own internal code, but many do not for reasons of efficiency. Some OSes partially make the division. Some common true window managers include CDE (Common Desktop Environment), GNOME, KDE, Aqua, OpenWindows, Motif, FVWM, Sugar, and Enlightenment. Some common hybrid window managers with OS extensions include Windows ME, Windows 98, Windows 95, Windows 3.1, OS/2 and GEOS.

Windows '95

Windows '95 is currently the second most popular variant of MS-Windows. It was designed to be the replacement Windows 3.1 but has not yet done so completely partly because of suspected security problems but even more because it is not as lightweight and will not work on all the machines that Windows 3.1 will. It is more capable than Windows 3.1 though and now has excellent driver support and more games available for it than any other platform. It is made to run on top of MS-DOS and will not do much of anything if MS-DOS is not on the system. It is thus not strictly an OS per se, but nor is it a true window manager either; rather the combination of MS-DOS and Windows '95 result in a full OS with GUI. It is partially multitasking but has a much greater chance of crashing than Windows NT does (or probably even Mac OS) if faced with a buggy program. Windows '95 runs only on x86 based machines. Currently Windows '95 has several Y2K issues, some of which have patches that can be downloaded for free, and some of which do not yet have fixes at all.

Windows '98

Windows '98 is quite possibly the second most popular form of MS-Windows, in spite of the fact that its official release is currently a point of legal debate with at least nineteen states, the federal government, and a handful of foreign countries as it has a few questionable features that might restrict the novice computer user and/or unfairly compete with other computer companies. It also has some specific issues with the version of Java that comes prepackaged with it that has never been adequately fixed, and it still has several Y2K issues, most of which have patches that can be downloaded for free (in fact, Microsoft guarantees that it will work properly through 2000 with the proper patches), but some of which do not yet have fixes at all (it won't work properly through 2001 at this point). In any case, it was designed to replace Windows '95.

Windows 2000

Windows 2000 was the intended replacement for Windows NT and in that capacity received relatively lukewarm support. Being based on Windows NT, it inherits some of its driver support problems. Originally it was also supposed to replace Windows '98, but Windows ME was made to do that instead, and the merger between Windows NT and Windows '98 was postponed until Windows XP.

Windows 3.1

Windows 3.1 remains a surprisingly popular variant of MS-Windows. It is lighter weight than either Windows '95 or Windows NT (but not lighter weight than GEOS) but less capable than the other two. It is made to run on top of MS-DOS and will not do much of anything if MS-DOS is not on the system. It is thus not strictly an OS per se, but nor is it a true window manager, either; rather the combination of MS-DOS and Windows 3.1 result in a full OS with GUI. Its driver support is good, but its game selection is limited. Windows 3.1 runs only on x86 based machines. It has some severe Y2K issues that may or may not be fixed.

Windows CE

Windows CE is the lightweight variant of MS-Windows. It offers the general look and feel of Windows '95 but is targetted primarily for hand-held devices, PDAs, NCs, and embedded devices. It does not have all the features of either Windows '95 or Windows NT and is very different from Windows 3.1. In particular, it will not run any software made for any of the other versions of MS-Windows. Special versions of each program must be made. Furthermore, there are actually a few slightly different variants of Windows CE, and no variant is guaranteed to be able to run software made specifically for another one. Driver support is also fairly poor for all types, and few games are made for it. Windows CE will run on a few different processor types, including the x86 and several different processors dedicated to PDAs, embedded systems, and hand-held devices.

Windows ME

Windows ME is yet another flavor of MS-Windows (specifically the planned replacement for Windows '98). Windows ME currently runs only on the x86 processor.

Windows NT

Windows NT is the industrial-strength variant of MS-Windows. Current revisions offer the look and feel of Windows '95 and older revisions offer the look and feel of Windows 3.1. It is the most robust flavor of MS-Windows and is fully multitasking. It is also by far the most expensive flavor of MS-Windows and has far less software available for it than Windows '95 or '98. In particular, do not expect to play many games on a Windows NT machine, and expect some difficulty in obtaining good drivers. Windows NT will run on a few different processor types, including the x86, the Alpha, and the PowerPC. Plans are in place to port Windows NT to the Merced when it becomes available.

Windows Vista

Windows Vista is the newest flavor of MS-Windows (specifically the planned replacement for Windows XP). Windows Vista (originally known as Longhorn) currently only runs on x86 processors.

Windows XP

Windows XP is yet another flavor of MS-Windows (specifically the planned replacement for both Windows ME and Windows 2000). Windows XP currently only runs on the x86 processors. Windows XP is currently the most popular form of MS-Windows.

WinTel

An x86 based system running some flavor of MS-Windows.

workstation

Depending upon whom you ask, a workstation is either an industrial strength desktop computer or its own category above the desktops. Workstations typically have some flavor of UNIX for their OS, but there has been a recent trend to call high-end Windows NT and Windows 2000 machines workstations, too.

WYSIWYG

What you see is what you get; an adjective applied to a program that attempts to exactly represent printed output on the screen. Related to WYSIWYM but quite different.

WYSIWYM

What you see is what you mean; an adjective applied to a program that does not attempt to exactly represent printed output on the screen, but rather defines how things are used and so will adapt to different paper sizes, etc. Related to WYSIWYG but quite different.

X-Face

X-Faces are small monochrome images embedded in headers for both provides a e-mail and news messages. Better mail and news applications will display them (sometimes automatically, sometimes only per request).

X-Windows

X-Windows provides a GUI for most UNIX systems, but can also be found as an add-on library for other computers. Numerous window managers run on top of it. It is often just called "X".

X3D

Extensible **3D** Graphics data is an XML file that is used to hold three-dimensional graphical data. It is the successor to VRML.

x86

The x86 series of processors includes the Pentium, Pentium Pro, Pentium II, Pentium III, Celeron, and Athlon as well as the 786, 686, 586, 486, 386, 286, 8086, 8088, etc. It is an exceptionally popular design (by far the most popular CISC series) in spite of the fact that even its fastest model is significantly slower than the assorted RISC processors. Many different OSes run on machines built around x86 processors, including MS-DOS, Windows 3.1, Windows '95, Windows '98, Windows ME, Windows NT, Windows 2000, Windows CE, Windows XP, GEOS, Linux, Solaris, OpenBSD, NetBSD, FreeBSD, Mac OS X, OS/2, BeOS, CP/M, etc. A couple different companies produce x86 processors, but the bulk of them are produced by Intel. It is expected that this processor will eventually be completely replaced by the Merced, but the Merced development schedule is somewhat behind. Also, it should be noted that the Pentium III processor has stirred some controversy by including a "fingerprint" that will enable individual computer usage of web pages etc. to be accurately tracked.

XBL

An XML Binding Language document is used to associate executable content with an XML tag. It is itself an XML file, and is used most frequently (although not exclusively) in conjunction with XUL.

XHTML

The Extensible Hypertext Mark-up Language is essentially a cleaner, stricter version of HTML. It is a proper subset of XML.

XML

The Extensible Mark-up Language is a subset of SGML and a superset of XHTML. It is used for numerous things including (among many others) RSS and RDF.

XML-RPC

XML-RPC provides a fairly lightweight means by which one computer can execute a program on a co-operating machine across a network like the Internet. It is based on XML and is used for everything from fetching stock quotes to checking weather forcasts.

XO

The energy-efficient, kid-friendly laptop produced by the OLPC project. It runs Sugar for its window manager and Linux for its OS. It sports numerous built-in features like wireless networking, a video camera & microphone, a few USB ports, and audio in/out jacks. It comes with several educational applications (which it refers to as "Activities"), most of which are written in Python.

XSL

The Extensible Stylesheet Language is like CSS for XML. It provides a means of describing how an XML resource should be displayed.

XSLT

XSL Transformations are used to transform one type of XML into another. It is a component of XSL that can be (and often is) used independently.

XUL

An XML User-Interface Language document is used to define a user interface for an application using XML to specify the individual controls as well as the overall layout.

Y2K

The general class of problems resulting from the wrapping of computers' internal date timers is given this label in honor of the most obvious occurrence -- when the year changes from 1999 to 2000 (abbreviated in some programs as 99 to 00 indicating a backwards time movement). Contrary to popular belief, these problems will not all manifest themselves on the first day of 2000, but will in fact happen over a range of dates extending out beyond 2075. A computer that does not have problems prior to the beginning of 2001 is considered "Y2K compliant", and a computer that does not have problems within the next ten years or so is considered for all practical purposes to be "Y2K clean". Whether or not a given computer is "clean" depends upon both its OS and its applications (and in some unfortunate cases, its hardware). The quick rundown on common home / small business machines (roughly from best to worst) is that:

All Mac OS systems are okay until at least the year 2040. By that time a patch should be available.

All BeOS systems are okay until the year 2040 (2038?). By that time a patch should be available.

Most UNIX versions are either okay or currently have free fixes available (and typically would not have major problems until 2038 or later in any case).

NewtonOS has a problem with the year 2010, but has a free fix available.

Newer AmigaOS systems are okay; older ones have a problem with the year 2000 but have a free fix available. They also have a year 2077 problem that does not yet have a free fix.

Some OS/2 systems have a year 2000 problem, but free fixes are available.

All CP/M versions have a year 2000 problem, but free fixes are available.

PC-DOS has a year 2000 problem, but a free fix is available.

DR-DOS has a year 2000 problem, but a free fix is available.

Different versions of GEOS have different problems ranging from minor year 2000 problems (with fixes in the works) to larger year 2080 problems (that do not have fixes yet). The only problem that may not have a fix in time is the year 2000 problem on the Apple][version of GEOS; not only was that version discontinued, unlike the other GEOS versions it no longer has a parent company to take care of it.

All MS-Windows versions (except possibly Windows 2000 and Windows ME) have multiple problems with the year 2000 and/or 2001, most of which have free fixes but some of which still lack free fixes as of this writing. Even new machines off the shelf that are labelled "Y2K Compliant" usually are not unless additional software is purchased and installed. Basically WinNT and WinCE can be properly patched, Windows '98 can be patched to work properly through 2000 (possibly not 2001), Windows '95 can be at least partially patched for 2000 (but not 2001) but is not being guaranteed by Microsoft, and Windows 3.1 cannot be fully patched.

MS-DOS has problems with at least the year 2000 (and probably more). None of its problems have been addressed as of this writing. Possible fixes are to change over to either PC-DOS or DR-DOS.

Results vary wildly for common applications, so it is better to be safe than sorry and check out the ones that you use. It should also be noted that some of the biggest expected Y2K problems will be at the two ends of the computer spectrum with older legacy mainframes (such as power some large banks) and some of the various tiny embedded computers (such as power most burglar alarms and many assorted appliances). Finally, it should also be mentioned that some older WinTel boxes and Amigas may have Y2K problems in their hardware requiring a card addition or replacement.

Z-Machine

A virtual machine optimized for running interactive fiction, interactive tutorials, and other interactive things of a primarily textual nature. Z-Machines have been ported to almost every platform in use today. Z-machine bytecode is usually called Z-code. The Glulx virtual machine is of the same idea but somewhat more modern in concept.

Z80

The Z80 series of processors is a CISC design and is not being used in too many new stand-alone computer systems, but can still be occasionally found in embedded systems. It is the most popular processor for CP/M machines.

Zaurus

The Zaurus is a brand of PDA. It is generally in between a Palm and a Newton in capability.

zip

There are three common zips in the computer world that are completely different from one another. One is a type of removable removable disk slightly larger (physically) and vastly larger (capacity) than a floppy. The second is a group of programs used for running interactive fiction. The third is a group of programs used for compression.

Zoomer

The Zoomer is a type of PDA. Zoomers all use GEOS for their OS and are / were produced by numerous different companies and are thus found under numerous different names. The "classic" Zoomers are known as the Z-7000, the Z-PDA, and the GRiDpad and were made by Casio, Tandy, and AST respectively. Newer Zoomers include HP's OmniGo models, Hyundai's Gulliver (which may not have actually been released to the general public), and Nokia's Communicator line of PDA / cell phone hybrids.
